Favourite
Mince Recipes

Favourite Mince Recipes

Lee Blaylock

First published in the UK in 2010 by
Apple Press
7 Greenland Street
London NW1 0ND
United Kingdom

www.apple-press.com

Isbn 978-1-84543-391-8

First published in Australia in 2010 by
Penguin Group (Australia)
250 Camberwell Road
Camberwell
Victoria 3124
Australia
(a division of Pearson Australia Group Pty Ltd

Cover and text design by Marley Flory © Penguin Group (Australia)
Photography by Paul Nelson
Food styling by Rebecca Quinn
Typeset in AkzidenzGrotesk by Post Pre-press Group, Brisbane, Queensland
Scanning and separations by Splitting Image P/L, Clayton, Victoria
Printed and bound in China by Everbest Printing Co. Ltd

penguin.com.au

Contents

Introduction

Versatile, delicious and economical. There's never been a better time to discover the delights of cooking with mince. Get ready to throw out any preconceived notions you may have that mince is an old-fashioned or humdrum ingredient – with this book you'll discover just how flavoursome, easy-to-use and endlessly versatile mince can be.

Inside this cookbook you will find over 100 tasty meals that use different types of mince ranging from beef, chicken and pork to fish. The ingredients listed in each recipe are kitchen basics or can easily be bought from various supermarkets, delicatessens or local markets.

So, what exactly *is* mince? Meat mince is basically very finely chopped or ground meat; usually made from cuts such as the leg, shoulder or rump. Meat grinders are available for domestic use so you can make your own mince at home.

Fish mince is made by blending fresh, firm fish in a food processor. It is a great way to incorporate fish into your daily diet, especially paired with interesting Asian flavours such as curry paste, kaffir lime leaves and peanuts.

Mince can also be purchased from the supermarket or your local butcher. For a finer mince, ask your butcher to put the meat through the grinder a second time or, if you are making your own, use the finest hole of the meat grinder.

To store mince, place it in a clean bowl and cover it tightly with cling wrap. Store in the fridge for up to four days. Fish mince will keep for up to three days. Alternatively, you can freeze mince meat in freezer bags for up to three months. Flatten the mince slightly in each bag before freezing as this will quicken the defrosting process later on. To defrost the meat, place it, in the freezer bag, on a clean plate and leave overnight in the refrigerator.

This cookbook also includes recipes that use fruit mince. This ingredient is especially popular at Christmas-time for making delicious mince pies.

Whatever its form, mince can be as exciting as you wish to make it. It's also a great way to keep grocery costs down. With so many ways to use mince – dumplings, soups, meatballs, pasta bakes and desserts – it never gets boring. There's almost nothing mince can't do!

Starters

Beef Party Pies

1 tablespoon olive oil
1 brown onion, finely diced
1 zucchini, grated
1 carrot, grated
1 tablespoon dried mixed herbs
500 g beef mince
1 tablespoon plain flour
1 cup beef stock
2 sheets shortcrust pastry
2 sheets puff pastry
1 egg, beaten, for glazing
chutney or tomato sauce, to serve

Preheat oven to 180°C. Lightly grease 2 × 12-hole mini-muffin pans.

Heat oil in a large non-stick frying pan over medium heat. Add the onion and sauté for 2 minutes until soft and golden. Add the zucchini, carrot and mixed herbs and cook for a further minute. Add the beef mince to the pan using a wooden spoon to break up any lumps. Cook for 5 minutes then stir through the flour, and add the beef stock. Cook uncovered for 15 minutes.

Cut the shortcrust pastry sheets into 18 even squares. Line the muffin pans with the shortcrust pastry squares. Spoon mince mixture evenly among pastry cases.

Cut the puff pastry sheets into 18 even squares. Top each pie with a pastry square. Use a small sharp knife to trim excess pastry. Brush tops with beaten egg.

Place in the preheated oven and bake for 20 minutes or until golden-brown. Remove from oven and set aside to cool.

Serve with chutney or tomato sauce.

MAKES 18

Mini Sausage Rolls with Plum Sauce

½ cup soft breadcrumbs
⅓ cup milk
250 g pork mince
250 g chicken mince
½ small onion, finely chopped
1 egg
1 tablespoon finely chopped fresh
    flat-leaf parsley
1 tablespoon finely chopped fresh
    sage or thyme
freshly ground black pepper
2 sheets puff pastry
1 egg, lightly beaten, for glazing
sesame seeds
plum sauce, to serve

Place breadcrumbs and milk in a bowl and leave for 5 minutes until milk is absorbed.

Place mince in a blender or food processor with the soaked breadcrumbs, onion and egg. Process until well combined. Stir fresh herbs and ground pepper through the mixture, cover, and refrigerate for 30 minutes.

Place one sheet of pastry on a lightly floured surface and cut lengthways in two. Spoon a quarter of the filling along the centre of each pastry strip, and brush one long edge with beaten egg. Fold pastry over and roll up to form a log. Repeat, to make four logs.

Preheat oven to 180°C. Line a large baking tray with non-stick baking paper.

Place logs on tray. Glaze top with beaten egg and sprinkle with sesame seeds. Cut each log into ten (this makes quite small rolls). Place trays in oven and bake for 20–25 minutes until pastry is puffed and golden-brown.

Serve warm with plum sauce.

MAKES 40

Oriental Beef Balls

1 cup soft breadcrumbs
1 cup milk
1 kg good-quality beef mince
1 onion, finely chopped
2 tablespoons finely chopped fresh
  coriander
1 tablespoon finely grated fresh
  ginger
1 egg, lightly beaten
salt and freshly ground black pepper
1 cup sesame seeds
sweet chilli sauce, to serve

Preheat over to 180°C. Lightly oil a non-stick baking tray.

Soak the breadcrumbs in the milk for about 10 minutes. Drain, and squeeze out milk (the bread will be pulpy). Place bread, mince, onion, coriander, ginger and egg in a bowl and mix well. Season with salt and pepper.

Shape mixture into small, bite-size balls and roll these lightly in sesame seeds. Place on prepared tray and bake in preheated oven for about 20 minutes until golden on the outside and cooked through.

Serve hot, with sweet chilli sauce for dipping.

MAKES 24

Prawn & Ginger Dumplings

400 g raw prawn meat
1 tablespoon grated ginger
1 tablespoon freshly squeezed
    lime juice
2 kaffir lime leaves, finely shredded
salt and finely ground black pepper
25 dumpling wrappers
2 cups fish stock
sweet chilli sauce, to serve

Place the prawns, ginger, lime juice and lime leaves in a food processor, blend until combined. Season with salt and pepper.

On a clean surface, lay out a dumpling wrapper.

Place a tablespoonful of the prawn mixture onto a wrapper, brush the edge with water and seal together. Repeat with the remaining mixture and wrappers.

Bring the stock to the boil in a saucepan and reduce heat to simmer. Cook the dumplings in batches, about 4 minutes at a time, until they are cooked through.

Serve hot with sweet chilli sauce on the side.

SERVES 4

Naam Phrik (Spicy Thai Relish)

Paste

4 long fresh red chillies, deseeded,
  chopped
1 stem lemongrass, finely chopped
½ red onion, chopped
2 cloves garlic, chopped
2 tomatoes, roughly chopped

2 tablespoons vegetable oil
200 g pork mince
2 tablespoons fish sauce
1 teaspoon sugar

To make the paste, combine all ingredients in a food processor and blend well.

Heat oil in a non-stick frying pan over medium heat. Add the paste and fry until fragrant (about 2 minutes). Add the pork mince to the pan and cook for 5 minutes, breaking up any lumps with a wooden spoon.

Season with fish sauce and sugar and add a little water to moisten if needed.

To serve

Serve with blanched vegetables such as green beans or cabbage.

SERVES 4

Pork, Prawn & Lemongrass Wontons

350 g pork mince

150 g raw (green) prawns, shelled
and deveined and finely chopped
(or pulse in food processor)

1 × 225-g can water chestnuts,
drained and finely chopped

1 tablespoon grated fresh ginger

2 tablespoons peeled and finely
chopped lemongrass

1 teaspoon chilli jam

2 teaspoons soft brown sugar

2 egg yolks, beaten

1 packet wonton wrappers

chopped chives, to serve

Dipping Sauce

½ cup soy sauce

1 teaspoon sesame oil

½ teaspoon grated fresh ginger

½ teaspoon finely sliced fresh
red chilli

To make dipping sauce, place all ingredients in a small bowl and whisk until combined. Set aside until needed.

To make wonton filling, place mince, prawns, water chestnuts, ginger, lemongrass, chilli jam, sugar and egg yolks in a bowl. Mix until combined.

Place 1 teaspoonful of the mixture in the centre of a wonton wrapper. Moisten edges with water, pull up sides to form a small bundle, twist, and press to keep together. (As you work, keep the wonton wrappers and wontons covered with a damp tea towel to prevent them drying out.) Repeat with remaining mixture.

Place wontons on a tray, cover and refrigerate until ready to use.

Lightly oil the slats of a bamboo steamer or line with non-stick baking paper. Half-fill a large saucepan or wok with boiling water. Place wontons in the steamer (in two or three batches, depending on size of steamer), leaving some space between them. Place steamer over saucepan or wok, cover, and steam for 7–8 minutes until wontons are firm.

To serve

Transfer cooked wontons to a serving platter, sprinkle with chopped chives and serve immediately with the dipping sauce on the side.

MAKES 35–40

Scotch Eggs

7 eggs
plain flour, to dust
1 onion, chopped
2 cloves garlic, crushed
2 tablespoons chopped fresh flat-leaf
    parsley
500 g beef mince
salt and freshly ground black pepper
2 cups dry breadcrumbs
vegetable oil, for deep frying

Place 6 eggs in a saucepan of cold water. Bring to the boil turn heat down to simmer and cook for 8–10 minutes. Drain and set aside to cool completely.

Once cooled, peel the eggs carefully and dust with flour.

Place the onion, garlic, parsley and beef mince into a food processor. Blend until combined. Add the remaining egg and process until the mixture comes together. Season with salt and pepper.

Divide the mixture into six even portions.

Place breadcrumbs in bowl.

Mould one portion of the mince around 1 egg and shape the meat around to enclose. Coat in breadcrumbs and set aside. Repeat with the other eggs.

Heat oil in a large saucepan for deep-frying. Drop a piece of bread into the oil to test if it is hot enough, the bread should turn golden. Place 2 eggs carefully in the oil and fry for 10 minutes, until golden-brown. Place on a plate lined with paper towel to drain excess oil. Repeat with the remaining eggs.

Serve warm.

SERVES 3–6

Shanghai Chicken Dumplings

3 dried shiitake mushrooms

250 g chicken mince

2 water chestnuts (drain if canned),
   finely chopped

3 tablespoons finely sliced spring
   onion

1 tablespoon grated fresh ginger

1 clove garlic, crushed

1 tablespoon finely sliced fresh
   red chilli

1 tablespoon soy sauce

1 teaspoon sesame oil

salt and white pepper

25 round gow-gee wrappers

Dipping Sauce

½ cup soy sauce

2 tablespoons mirin (rice wine)
   or dry sherry

1 teaspoon sesame oil

1 teaspoon finely grated ginger

To make dipping sauce, combine all ingredients in a small bowl and stir until mixed. Cover and set aside until needed.

Put dried mushrooms in a small bowl, cover with boiling water and soak for 15 minutes. Drain, squeeze out any excess moisture and chop flesh finely (if stalks are tough, remove and discard).

Place chicken, water chestnuts, spring onion, ginger, garlic, chilli, soy, sesame oil, salt and pepper in a bowl, and mix until combined. Cover and refrigerate for at least 30 minutes.

Place a small spoonful of the chicken mixture in the centre of a gow-gee wrapper. Moisten edges with water and fold over into a semi-circle. Pinch the edges together, then stand the dumpling on its base with the frill at the top. Keep wrappers and finished dumplings under a damp tea towel as you work, to avoid them drying out.

Lightly oil the base of a large bamboo steamer. Half fill a wok or pot with boiling water, place dumplings in the steamer (in batches) and steam for 7–8 minutes. Remove and serve with the dipping sauce.

MAKES 25

Keftedes with Mint Yoghurt

1 kg lean beef mince
½ cup soft breadcrumbs
½ onion, finely chopped
1 clove garlic, crushed
1 tablespoon dried oregano
½ cup crumbled fetta cheese
1 egg, beaten
freshly ground black pepper
olive oil, for shallow frying

Mint Yoghurt

1 cup Greek-style yoghurt
2 tablespoons finely chopped
   fresh mint leaves
1 tablespoon freshly squeezed
   lemon juice
salt

To make the mint yoghurt, mix all ingredients well, cover, and refrigerate for at least 30 minutes before serving.

To make keftedes, combine all the ingredients in a large bowl except the oil and mix well to combine. Cover mixture and refrigerate for half an hour.

Using wet hands, shape mixture into small balls. Heat about 2 cm of oil in a non-stick frying pan over medium heat. When it is hot, cook meatballs in batches until golden-brown and crisp all over (5–7 minutes, depending on size). Drain on paper towel.

To serve

Serve the keftedes hot or at room temperature, with mint yoghurt in small bowls for dipping.

MAKES 20–30

Pork Spring Rolls

50 g vermicelli noodles
350 g pork mince
2 shiitake mushrooms, finely chopped
1 carrot, peeled, grated
2 spring onions, thinly sliced
2 cloves garlic, crushed
1 tablespoon fish sauce
2 teaspoons caster sugar
20 spring-roll wrappers
vegetable oil, for deep frying
lettuce leaves, to serve
cucumber, cut into batons to serve
mint leaves, to serve

Place the noodles in a bowl and cover with boiling water. Set aside for 10 minutes or until the noodles are tender. Drain and cut the noodles into short lengths. Place in a large bowl and add the pork mince, mushrooms, carrot, spring onions, garlic, fish sauce and sugar. Mix well to combine.

To make the dipping sauce mix all ingredients in a bowl and stir until combined. Set aside.

Place a spring-roll wrapper on a clean work surface. Place a heaped teaspoonful of the mixture onto the centre of the wrapper. Fold in the sides and roll up tightly to enclose the filling. Place, seam-side down, on a baking tray and cover with a damp tea towel. Repeat with remaining mixture and wrappers.

Continued >

Dipping Sauce

¼ cup fish sauce

1 long fresh red chilli, deseeded,
   finely chopped

2 cloves garlic, crushed

2 tablespoons water

2 tablespoons freshly squeezed
   lime juice

1 tablespoon rice wine vinegar

1 tablespoon caster sugar

Heat oil in a large saucepan for deep-frying. Drop a piece of bread into the oil to test if it is hot enough, the bread should turn golden. Add 5 spring rolls to the oil and cook for 2–3 minutes or until golden-brown. Repeat with remaining spring rolls.

To serve

Serve with the dipping sauce, lettuce, cucumber and mint leaves. Each spring roll should be rolled up in a lettuce leaf with cucumber and mint, and then dipped into the dipping sauce.

SERVES 4

Gyoza

250 g pork mince
1 cup finely shredded cabbage
¼ cup finely chopped chives
1 clove garlic, crushed
1 tablespoon light soy sauce
1 tablespoon grated ginger
1 teaspoon sesame oil
¼ teaspoon ground pepper
30 gyoza wrappers
2 tablespoons vegetable oil

Dipping Sauce

1 tablespoon light soy
1 tablespoon rice vinegar
1 teaspoon caster sugar
1 teaspoon sesame oil

Combine the pork mince, cabbage, chives, garlic, soy sauce, ginger, sesame oil and pepper in a bowl. Mix thoroughly to combine.

Place a gyoza wrapper on a clean work surface. Place a heaped teaspoonful of the pork mixture onto the centre of the wrapper. Brush the edge with a little water. Bring the edges up to meet and use your fingertips to pleat the edge 4–5 times. Continue with the remaining mixture and wrappers.

To make the dipping sauce, mix the soy sauce, rice vinegar, 1 tablespoon water, sugar and sesame oil in a small bowl.

Heat oil in a large non-stick frying pan over high heat. Cook the dumplings for 2 minutes until the base of each gyoza is golden. Sprinkle ½ cup water over the gyoza, cover and cook for 3–4 minutes or until the water evaporates and the gyoza are firm.

Serve with the dipping sauce.

SERVES 6

Steamed Pork Dim Sum

250 g pork mince
1 small fresh red chilli, finely chopped
1 clove garlic, crushed
1 tablespoon grated ginger
2 tablespoons chopped fresh
    coriander leaves
2 tablespoons hoisin sauce
1 tablespoon water chestnuts
1 teaspoon fish sauce
30 dumpling wrappers
1 egg, beaten
dipping sauce, to serve

Place the pork mince, chilli, garlic, ginger, coriander, hoisin sauce, water chestnuts and fish sauce in a food processor and process until combined.

Place a dumpling wrapper on a clean surface. Place a heaped teaspoonful of the pork mixture into the centre of the wrapper. Brush the edge of the wrapper with egg and bring up to tightly enclose the filling. Repeat with the remaining mixture.

Line a large steamer basket with baking paper. Arrange the dim sum in the basket. Cover and steam for 8–10 minutes or until firm.

Serve with a dipping sauce of your choice.

SERVES 6

Thai Chicken & Coconut Pies

1 tablespoon vegetable oil

350 g chicken mince

1 clove garlic, crushed

⅓ cup coconut milk

2 tablespoons sweet chilli sauce

2 teaspoons lemongrass, peeled and
finely chopped

1 tablespoon freshly squeezed lime
juice

1 teaspoon finely grated lime zest

2 tablespoons finely chopped fresh
coriander leaves

4 sheets puff pastry

1 egg, lightly beaten, to glaze

1 tablespoon sesame seeds

Heat oil in a large, non-stick frying pan over medium heat. Add chicken mince and cook, stirring, for 6–7 minutes until lightly browned. Allow to cool.

Combine chicken with garlic, coconut milk, chilli sauce, lemongrass, lime juice and zest, and coriander. Mix well, cover, and refrigerate for at least 15 minutes.

Preheat oven to 220°C. Lightly oil a non-stick, 12-hole muffin pan.

Cut 12 rounds of pastry 8.5-cm wide, and 12 rounds 6.5-cm wide. Fit the large rounds into muffin holes and press lightly. Fill each pastry cup with chicken mixture, then top with the smaller pastry rounds, pressing edges to seal.

Brush pies with the beaten egg, cut a small slit in the centre of each lid, and sprinkle pies with sesame seeds. Place in the preheated oven and bake for 25 minutes, or until golden-brown and puffed on top.

Serve hot or warm.

MAKES 12

San Choy Bao

1 tablespoon sunflower oil

1 clove garlic, crushed

2 spring onions, chopped

1 teaspoon finely grated fresh ginger

1 tablespoon sesame seeds

½ cup chopped water chestnuts

500 g pork mince

1 tablespoon kecap manis (sweet
   soy sauce)

2 tablespoons oyster sauce

16 baby cos lettuce leaves

2 spring onions, finely sliced on
   an angle

Heat oil over medium-high heat in a non-stick frying pan or wok. Add garlic, spring onions, ginger and sesame seeds, and fry for 1–2 minutes until fragrance is released. Add water chestnuts and pork mince, and stir-fry until mince is well browned (about 4–5 minutes). Add kecap manis and oyster sauce, reduce heat and simmer for 5 minutes.

Trim lettuce leaves if necessary to get an even size.

To serve

Arrange lettuce 'cups' on a platter and spoon in the mince. Sprinkle with spring onions and serve immediately.

MAKES 16

Mains

Seafood

Thai Fish Cakes
with Carrot & Herb Salad

500 g firm white boneless fish

2 tablespoons red curry paste

1 fresh red chilli, deseeded

2 tablespoons fish sauce

1 egg

1 teaspoon white sugar

1 tablespoon chopped coriander
   leaves

2 snake beans, chopped

2 spring-onion whites, thinly sliced

2 kaffir lime leaves, finely shredded

3 carrots, grated

½ red onion, thinly sliced

¼ cup roughly chopped mint leaves

½ cup roughly chopped coriander
   leaves

½ bunch chives, chopped

1 cup bean shoots

1 tablespoon sesame seeds

2 tablespoons white vinegar

1 tablespoon sesame oil

1 cup vegetable oil

sweet chilli sauce, to serve

Place the fish, curry paste, chilli, fish sauce, egg and sugar in a food processor. Blend until well combined and transfer to a bowl. Add the coriander, beans, spring-onion whites and kaffir lime leaves. Mix thoroughly to combine.

Roll 2 tablespoonfuls of fish mixture into balls and flatten slightly. Place on a tray and refrigerate for 1 hour.

In a large bowl gently toss together the carrot, red onion, mint, coriander, chives, bean shoots, sesame seeds, vinegar and sesame oil. Set aside.

Heat vegetable oil in a frying pan to high heat and shallow fry the fish cakes in batches until golden all over.

To serve

Place the prepared salad on plates and top with the fish cakes. Serve with a side of sweet chilli sauce.

SERVES 4

Coconut Soup with Fish Dumplings

500 g firm white boneless fish

1 tablespoon grated ginger

1 tablespoon chopped coriander
   leaves

1 fresh red chilli, chopped

2 cups coconut milk

3 cups vegetable stock

2 tablespoons fish sauce

1 tablespoon sugar

2 stems lemongrass, bruised and
   chopped into large pieces

¼ cup freshly squeezed lime juice

2 long fresh red chillies, deseeded
   and chopped

2-cm piece ginger, peeled and sliced

½ cup coriander leaves

Place the fish, ginger, coriander and chilli into a food processor and blend until combined. Roll tablespoonfuls of the mixture into balls and set aside.

In a large saucepan combine coconut milk, stock, fish sauce, sugar, lemongrass, lime juice, chilli and ginger. Bring to the boil, then reduce heat and simmer for 5 minutes. Add the fish dumplings and cook for a further 10 minutes.

Check seasoning and stir through the coriander leaves. Serve.

SERVES 4

Fish Burger

500 g firm white boneless fish

1 egg

2 tablespoons chopped fresh flat-leaf
parsley

1 clove garlic, crushed

1 tablespoon finely grated lemon zest

salt and freshly ground black pepper

½ cup parmesan cheese

1½ cups soft breadcrumbs

plain flour, to dust

1 egg, beaten

oil, for frying

4 lettuce leaves

4 crusty bread rolls

mayonnaise or tartar sauce

2 tomatoes, sliced

4 lemon wedges

Preheat oven to 180°C. Line a baking tray with baking paper.

Place the fish, egg, parsley, garlic and lemon zest into a food processor. Blend until combined. Season with salt and pepper.

Divide the mixture into four and shape into patties.

In a shallow bowl mix together the breadcrumbs and parmesan. Place flour in a separate bowl.

Dust each patty with flour, dip into the beaten egg and coat well in the breadcrumbs.

Heat oil in a large frying pan and brown the fish patties on both sides (about 3–4 minutes), place on the prepared tray and bake in the oven for 10–15 minutes until golden-brown.

To serve

Cut the bread rolls in half horizontally, place lettuce on the bottom half of each roll. Top with tomato, a fish patty and mayonnaise or tartar sauce. Close with top of bread roll. Serve with a lemon wedge on the side.

SERVES 4

Saffron Fish Balls

500 g firm white boneless fish
3 spring onions, chopped
¼ cup coriander leaves
¼ cup soft breadcrumbs
pinch of saffron threads, soaked
    in 1 tablespoon hot water
1 egg
salt and freshly ground black pepper
2 tablespoons olive oil
1 onion, finely chopped
1 teaspoon ground paprika
1 teaspoon Harissa paste
1 teaspoon ground cumin
1 teaspoon sugar
1 × 400-g can chopped tomatoes
1 cup vegetable stock
¼ cup chopped fresh flat-leaf parsley

Place the fish, spring onions, coriander, breadcrumbs, saffron threads and water, and egg into a food processor. Blend until combined. Season with salt and pepper.

Roll tablespoonfuls of the mixture into balls. Set aside.

Heat oil in a large saucepan over medium heat, add the onion and sauté until softened. Add the paprika, Harissa, cumin and sugar. Cook until fragrant.

Add tomatoes and stock and bring to the boil. Cover and simmer for 10–15 minutes. Add the fish balls and continue cooking for a further 15 minutes. Stir through the parsley. Serve warm.

SERVES 4

Indian Fish Cakes

400 g firm white boneless fish

2 medium potatoes, peeled, boiled
  and chopped

⅓ cup oil

1 onion, finely diced

2 cloves garlic, crushed

1 tablespoon grated ginger

1 long fresh green chilli, deseeded
  and chopped

½ teaspoon ground turmeric

1 teaspoon ground coriander

2 teaspoons garam masala

½ teaspoon ground chilli

2 tablespoons chopped coriander
  leaves

salt and freshly ground black pepper

naan bread, to serve

lime wedges, to serve

natural yoghurt, to serve

Preheat oven to 180°C. Line a baking tray with baking paper.

Place the fish and potato into a food processor and blend until combined.

Heat 2 tablespoons oil in a large non-stick frying pan. Add onion and garlic and sauté until softened. Add the ginger, green chilli, turmeric, coriander, garam masala and chilli. Cook until fragrant (about 1–2 minutes).

Stir through the fresh coriander. Transfer to a large bowl and add the fish and potato. Mix thoroughly to combine. Season with salt and pepper.

Divide the mixture into eight and roll into balls and flatten.

Heat remaining oil in a large non-stick frying pan and brown the fish cakes on both sides. Place cakes on the prepared tray and place in the oven to cook for 10–15 minutes.

To serve

Serve the fish cakes with naan bread, lime wedges and natural yoghurt.

SERVES 4

Tuna & Potato Cakes with Soft Boiled Egg

4 medium potatoes, peeled, boiled and chopped
400 g fresh tuna, chopped
2 tablespoons cream
½ red onion, chopped
1 tablespoon chopped fresh flat-leaf parsley
1 tablespoon chopped basil
6 eggs, 1 beaten
salt and freshly ground black pepper
plain flour, to dust
2 cups soft breadcrumbs
2 tablespoons vegetable oil
2 tablespoons wholegrain mustard
1 cup mayonnaise
2 tablespoons chopped chives
rocket leaves, to serve

Preheat oven to 180°C. Line a baking tray with baking paper.

Place the potato, tuna, cream, onion, parsley, basil and 1 egg in a food processor, blend until combined. Season with salt and pepper.

Divide the mixture into eight balls and flatten into cakes.

Place the beaten egg in a dish and the breadcrumbs in a separate dish. Dust each cake with flour, then dip into the egg and coat with breadcrumbs. Place the cakes on the prepared tray and set aside.

Place the remaining 4 eggs into a saucepan, cover with water and bring to the boil, reduce heat and simmer for 5 minutes. Run eggs under cold water and let cool completely.

Heat oil in an ovenproof pan, brown the tuna cakes on both sides, place pan in the oven to cook for 10–15 minutes.

Peel the eggs and cut in half.

Mix together the mustard and mayonnaise.

To serve

Serve the tuna cakes on a bed of rocket leaves with a soft-boiled egg and a dollop of mustard-mayonnaise.

SERVES 4

Seafood Agnolotti

200 g raw prawn meat
250 g firm white boneless fish
1 tablespoon grated lemon zest
1 cup cream
salt and freshly ground black pepper
500 g fresh pasta (or lasagne) sheets
½ cup white wine
1 tablespoon thyme leaves, plus extra
   for garnish

Lightly sprinkle flour onto a baking tray and set aside.

Place the prawn meat, fish, lemon zest and 2 tablespoons cream into a food processor. Blend until well combined. Season with salt and pepper.

Lay the pasta sheets out on a clean surface. Using a 10-cm fluted round cutter cut out approximately 30–40 circles.

Place a heaped teaspoonful of the seafood mixture onto each circle. Brush a little water around the outside of the circle and fold over to enclose. Seal the edges well making sure no air is trapped in the pocket. You should have semi-circles.

Place the agnolotti on the prepared baking tray and cover with a tea towel.

In a saucepan bring the remaining cream, wine and thyme leaves to the boil. Reduce heat and simmer for 5 minutes until thickened. Season with salt and pepper.

Meanwhile bring a large saucepan of salted water to the boil. Cook the pasta for 3–5 minutes, until al dente. The agnolotti will float to the surface when ready. Drain well and add to the cream sauce, toss to coat and heat through. Sprinkle with extra thyme leaves and serve.

SERVES 4

Prawn Balls with Green Curry

500 g raw prawn meat
⅓ cup green curry paste
1 × 400-ml can coconut cream
¼ cup freshly squeezed lime juice
1 tablespoon finely chopped
   lemongrass
1 teaspoon sugar
½ cup vegetable stock
¼ cup vegetable oil
¼ cup chopped coriander leaves
¼ cup chopped mint leaves
steamed rice, to serve

Place the prawn meat and 2 tablespoons curry paste into a food processor. Blend until combined.

Roll tablespoonfuls of mixture into balls.

In a saucepan combine the coconut cream, lime juice, lemongrass, sugar and stock. Gently bring to the boil, reduce heat and simmer for 5 minutes.

Heat oil in a non-stick frying pan and cook the fish balls until golden and crisp. Add to the coconut mixture, stir through the fresh herbs and serve with steamed rice.

SERVES 4

Salmon Cakes with Lemon

*500 g salmon fillet, bones and skin
  removed*
2 tablespoons cream
1 tablespoon grated ginger
¼ cup freshly squeezed lemon juice
1 tablespoon grated lemon zest
½ cup soft white breadcrumbs
salt and freshly ground black pepper
½ cup vegetable oil
lemon wedges, to serve

Preheat oven to 180°C.

Place the salmon and cream into a food processor and blend until just combined, leave the salmon a little chunky. Transfer to a bowl and stir through the ginger, lemon juice, zest and breadcrumbs. Season with salt and pepper.

Shape the mixture into eight portions and roll into balls and flatten slightly. (Dust hands with a little flour if the mix is too sticky.)

Heat oil in an ovenproof pan, brown the salmon cakes on both sides (about 3–4 minutes), place in the oven and cook for 10–15 minutes.

To serve

....

Serve with a side salad and lemon wedges.

SERVES 4

Prawn Cakes
with Cucumber Relish

500 g raw prawn meat
1 cup roughly chopped coriander
    leaves
2 cloves garlic, crushed
2 tablespoons grated ginger
⅓ cup light soy sauce
freshly ground black pepper
sugar
vegetable oil, for deep frying

Cucumber Relish

¼ cup white vinegar
¼ cup sugar
1 teaspoon salt
2 Lebanese cucumbers, diced
½ red onion, finely diced
1 tablespoon grated ginger
1 long fresh red chilli, chopped

Place the prawn meat, coriander, garlic, ginger and soy sauce in a processor and blend to combine. Season with pepper and sugar.

Divide mixture into eight balls and flatten into cakes.

To make the relish combine vinegar, sugar and salt in a saucepan. Bring to the boil and stir until the sugar dissolves. Set aside to cool.

Place the cucumber, onion, ginger and chilli in a bowl and pour in the syrup. Set aside.

Heat oil in a large saucepan for deep-frying. Place two prawn cakes in the oil and deep-fry until golden all over. Drain on paper towel. Repeat with the remaining prawn cakes.

To serve

Serve with a salad and the cucumber relish.

SERVES 4

Fish Skewers with Peanuts & Lime

500 g firm boneless fish fillets

1 tablespoon freshly squeezed
  lime juice

1 tablespoon grated lime zest

3 spring onions, finely sliced

1 long fresh green chilli

1 egg

2 tablespoons chopped coriander
  leaves

¼ cup chopped raw unsalted peanuts

¼ cup dry breadcrumbs

¼ cup vegetable oil

12 small bamboo skewers, soaked
  for 30 minutes

sweet chilli sauce, to serve

steamed rice, to serve

lime wedges, to serve

Place the fish, lime juice and zest, spring onions, chilli, egg, coriander, peanuts and breadcrumbs in a food processor and blend until well combined.

Divide the mixture into 12 even portions and shape firmly around the skewers.

Heat an oiled barbecue grill or a grill plate to high, brush the skewers with oil and cook on both sides for 5 minutes until golden.

To serve

Serve with chilli sauce, steamed rice and lime wedges.

SERVES 4

Homemade Baked Fish Fingers with Sweet Potato

2 large sweet potatoes
½ cup olive oil
salt and freshly ground black pepper
1 tablespoon thyme leaves
500 g firm boneless fish fillets
1 onion, finely diced
1 tablespoon freshly squeezed lemon juice
1 tablespoon grated lemon zest
2 potatoes, peeled, boiled, mashed
2 tablespoons chopped flat-leaf parsley
plain flour, to dust
2 eggs, beaten
2 cups panko crumbs

Preheat oven to 180°C. Line a baking tray with baking paper.

Cut the sweet potato into pieces. Place in a roasting tin, coat in 3 tablespoons oil and season with salt and pepper. Scatter over the thyme leaves. Place in the oven for 30 minutes until golden.

Place the fish, onion, lemon juice and zest in a food processor and blend until well combined. Transfer to a large bowl and season with salt and pepper. Add the mashed potatoes and parsley and mix thoroughly. Divide the mix into 12 portions and shape into fingers.

Place the flour, eggs and breadcrumbs in separate bowls. Dust each fish finger with flour, dip into the beaten eggs and coat well with the crumbs.

Heat the remaining oil in a large non-stick frying pan and brown the fish fingers on both sides until golden. Place on the prepared tray and place in the oven to cook for 10–15 minutes.

Serve with the roasted sweet potato.

SERVES 4

Chicken

Lap Chicken Salad

2 tablespoons vegetable oil

1 teaspoon grated ginger

1 stem lemongrass, finely chopped

2 kaffir lime leaves, shredded

1 fresh red chilli, chopped

400 g chicken mince

2 tablespoons chopped spring onions

3 tablespoons freshly squeezed lime
   juice

3 tablespoons fish sauce

3 tablespoons chopped coriander
   leaves

3 tablespoons chopped mint

½ cup bean sprouts

¼ Chinese cabbage, shredded

Heat oil in a large non-stick frying pan over medium heat. Add the ginger, lemongrass, half the lime leaves and chilli and cook for 1 minute. Add the chicken mince, stirring with a wooden spoon to break up any lumps. Reduce heat and simmer for 10 minutes until chicken mince has browned.

In a large bowl mix the remaining lime leaf, spring onions, lime juice, fish sauce and the cooked mince. Leave for 2–3 minutes to marinate slightly.

Stir through the coriander, mint, bean sprouts and shredded cabbage and serve.

SERVES 4

Chicken Bites with Plum Sauce

300 g lean chicken mince
60 g fresh soft breadcrumbs
2 tablespoons finely chopped fresh
*   coriander leaves*
1 tablespoon grated fresh ginger
4 spring onions, thinly sliced
1 egg
plum sauce, to serve

Preheat oven to 200°C. Lightly oil a baking tray.

Place chicken, breadcrumbs, coriander, ginger, onions and egg in a blender or food processor and pulse until combined.

Using wet hands, shape mixture into about ten small balls. Place on the prepared baking tray and refrigerate for 10 minutes.

Place chicken bites in the oven and bake for 20–25 minutes, turning once, until golden-brown.

To serve

Serve hot or cold, with plum sauce for dipping.

MAKES 10–12

Nasi Goreng with Chicken

1½ cups long-grain rice

3 tablespoons oyster sauce

⅓ cup tomato sauce

2 tablespoons soy sauce

1 teaspoon salt

2 tablespoons vegetable oil

350 g chicken mince

1 small onion, sliced

2 medium carrots cut into small strips

¼ Chinese cabbage, shredded

100 g green beans, sliced on the
    diagonal

4 eggs, fried, to serve

Cook the rice according to packet directions.

In a bowl, mix together the oyster, tomato and soy sauces and salt. Set aside.

Heat 1 tablespoon oil in a wok over medium-high heat. Add the chicken mince and cook for 5 minutes, stirring with a wooden spoon to break up any lumps. Remove mince from the pan and set aside.

Heat the remaining oil in the wok over medium-high heat. Add the onion and stir-fry for 1 minute, then add the carrots, cabbage, beans and stir-fry until the vegetables are soft but still have a crunch to them (about 3 minutes). Add the cooked chicken mince, rice and sauces to the wok.

Stir-fry until heated through and well combined (about 3–4 minutes).

Serve with a fried egg on top.

SERVES 4

Mini Chicken Meatballs in Vegetable Soup

2 tablespoons olive oil

1 large onion, diced

2 cloves garlic, chopped

2 medium carrots, diced

2 sticks celery, diced

2 zucchini, diced

1 bay leave

¼ cup fresh thyme leaves

6 cups chicken stock

400 g chicken mince

¾ cup soft breadcrumbs

1 cup grated parmesan cheese, plus
    extra to serve

3 tablespoons chopped fresh flat-leaf
    parsley

1 egg, beaten

salt and freshly ground black pepper

1 × 400-g can cannellini beans

Heat oil in a large saucepan over medium heat. Add onion and garlic and sauté until softened (about 2 minutes). Add carrots, celery, zucchini and bay leaf. Cook for a further 3–4 minutes until vegetables have softened. Add the thyme and stock. Bring to the boil, reduce heat and simmer for 40 minutes.

Meanwhile combine the chicken mince, breadcrumbs, parmesan cheese, parsley and egg together in a large bowl. Season with salt and pepper. Roll teaspoonfuls of mixture into balls.

Add the meatballs and cannellini beans to the soup and cook for a further 10 minutes until the meatballs change to a lighter colour and slightly shrink in size.

Serve soup in bowls topped with parmesan cheese.

SERVES 4–6

Clear Soup with Chicken Wontons

150 g chicken mince
3-cm piece fresh ginger, grated
4 spring onions, finely sliced
1 tablespoon chopped fresh coriander
    leaves
1 tablespoon soy sauce
250 g wonton wrappers
1 litre chicken stock
½ cup finely sliced spring onions,
    for garnish
extra soy sauce, to serve

In a small bowl combine chicken mince with ginger, spring onions, coriander and soy sauce.

Place a wonton wrapper on a clean surface. Place a teaspoonful of the mixture in the middle of the wrapper, wet edges, gather these in the middle and then pinch together to form a little pouch.

Repeat until all the chicken mixture has been used.

Bring chicken stock to the boil, add wontons, and simmer for 4–5 minutes, or until cooked through.

To serve

Serve in heated bowls, sprinkled with finely sliced spring onions and extra soy sauce on the side.

SERVES 4

Chicken Quesadilla with Guacamole

Guacamole

1 large ripe avocado
1 red onion, finely diced
2 cloves garlic, crushed
¼ cup freshly squeezed lemon juice
salt and freshly ground black pepper

1 tablespoon vegetable oil
1 onion, finely diced
1 clove garlic, crushed
2 teaspoons ground cumin
1 teaspoon ground coriander
1 teaspoon oregano
1 teaspoon ground chilli
1 teaspoon onion powder
400 g chicken mince
salt and freshly ground black pepper
8 soft tortillas
1½ cups grated mozzarella cheese
½ cup chopped jalapenos
2 medium tomatoes, diced
1 cup sour cream (optional)
shredded lettuce, to serve

Preheat oven to 180°C. Line a baking tray with baking paper.

To make the guacamole, place the avocado flesh into a bowl and mash with a fork until smooth. Add the onion, garlic and lemon juice, and mix well. Season with salt and pepper. Set aside.

Heat oil in a large non-stick frying pan. Add the onion and garlic and sauté until softened (about 2 minutes). Add the cumin, coriander, oregano, chilli and onion powder and cook for 2 minutes. Add the chicken mince to the pan, stirring with a wooden spoon to break up any lumps. Cook for 10 minutes, until the mince has browned. Season with salt and pepper.

Divide the chicken mixture into eight. Lay out the tortillas on a clean work surface. Place the mince on one half of each tortilla, top with the cheese, jalapenos and tomato. Fold each tortilla over to encase the filling. You should have half-circles.

Place the filled tortillas on the prepared tray and place in the oven for 10–15 minutes until the cheese has melted and the tortilla is crunchy.

To serve

Cut each tortilla in half and serve with guacamole, sour cream (if using) and lettuce.

SERVES 4–6

Turkish Pide with Chicken

3 cups plain flour

7 g-packet dried yeast

1 tablespoon salt

⅓ cup olive oil

1¼ cups lukewarm water

1 tablespoon natural yoghurt

1 onion, finely chopped

1 clove garlic, crushed

500 g chicken mince

½ teaspoon ground cinnamon

1 teaspoon mixed spice

1 tablespoon freshly squeezed lemon juice

2 tablespoons chopped fresh mint

2 tomatoes, diced

salt and freshly ground black pepper

Preheat oven to 200°C. Line two baking trays with baking paper.

Combine flour, yeast and salt in a bowl. Make a well in the centre and mix in 1 tablespoon oil, water and yoghurt until a soft dough forms. Turn dough out onto a clean, floured surface and knead for 5 minutes until dough is almost smooth.

Place the dough in a lightly greased bowl. Cover with cling wrap and leave in a warm place for 1 hour or until it has doubled in size.

Heat 2 tablespoons oil in a large non-stick frying pan. Add the onion and garlic and sauté until softened (about 2 minutes). Add the chicken mince, cinnamon, mixed spice, lemon juice and mint. Stir using a wooden spoon to break up any lumps. Cook for 15 minutes, adding a splash of water if the chicken is looking too dry. Add the chopped tomato. Season with salt and pepper and set aside.

Continued >

Once the dough has doubled in size, punch out the air with your fist. Turn dough onto a clean floured surface and knead for 1 minute. Cut dough in half and roll each half into an oval shape, about 1-cm thick.

Place the dough on the prepared baking trays. Divide the chicken mixture in half and place in the centre of each dough oval. Fold in the sides to partially enclose filling (do not completely close the pide). Pinch the dough together at each end, to form a boat shape.

Lightly brush each pide with remaining olive oil. Place in the oven and bake for 20 minutes until golden.

SERVES 4

Fajitas

1 tablespoon vegetable oil

1 large onion, sliced

2 cloves garlic, crushed

1 green capsicum, deseeded,
    thinly sliced

1 red capsicum, deseeded,
    thinly sliced

500 g chicken mince

¼ cup barbecue sauce

⅓ cup chilli sauce

2 teaspoons ground cumin

2 teaspoons ground coriander

salt and freshly ground black pepper

12 flour tortillas

guacamole (page 53)

1 cup sour cream

1 cup grated cheddar cheese

chunky salsa

lettuce, shredded, to serve

pickled jalapenos, chopped, to serve

Heat oil in a large non-stick frying pan. Add the onion and garlic and sauté until softened (about 2 minutes). Add the capsicum and cook for a further 5 minutes. Add the chicken mince, barbecue sauce, chilli sauce, cumin and coriander. Stir with a wooden spoon, breaking up any lumps. Cook for 10 minutes until the chicken has browned. Season with salt and pepper.

Heat tortillas in the microwave on HIGH for approximately 30 seconds. Wrap tortillas in a damp tea towel to keep them soft.

To serve

Place the chicken mixture, sour cream, cheddar cheese, salsa, lettuce and jalapenos in separate serving dishes. Place each serving dish on the table so fajitas can be assembled individually.

SERVES 4

Chicken Burgers
with Avocado Salsa

800 g chicken mince

1 clove garlic, crushed

1 small onion, finely chopped

⅓ cup shredded parmesan cheese

*1 tablespoon finely chopped fresh
thyme or oregano*

1 egg, beaten

½ cup soft breadcrumbs

salt and freshly ground black pepper

2 medium avocados, sliced

1 red onion, sliced

*2 tablespoons chopped fresh
coriander leaves*

*2 tablespoons baby capers, drained
and rinsed*

*2 tablespoons freshly squeezed
lemon juice*

½ cup olive oil

2 handfuls rocket leaves, to serve

6 crusty rolls or burger buns

Oil barbecue and preheat to medium-hot.

Combine chicken mince, garlic, onion, parmesan, thyme (or oregano), egg, breadcrumbs, salt and pepper in a large bowl. Mix well, then with wet hands shape into six patties.

Combine the sliced avocados and red onion in a medium-sized bowl with the chopped coriander and capers. Place the lemon juice and oil together in a screw-top jar, shake well, and set aside.

Cook chicken patties on preheated barbecue for 6–8 minutes on each side, until golden-brown and cooked through.

To serve

Place each patty in a roll, and top with rocket leaves and the avocado salsa. Drizzle with the dressing and serve at once.

SERVES 6

Chicken Skewers with Minted Yoghurt

500 g chicken mince

¼ cup chopped oregano leaves

juice and zest of 1 lemon

½ cup finely chopped flat-leaf parsley

50 g fetta cheese, crumbled

⅓ cup olive oil

salt and freshly ground black pepper

12 small bamboo skewers, soaked
   for 30 minutes

½ cup Greek-style yoghurt

2 tablespoons finely chopped mint

1 clove garlic, crushed

4 roma tomatoes, quartered

¼ cup pitted kalamata olives

2 tablespoons red wine vinegar

In a large bowl add the chicken mince, oregano, lemon juice and zest, ¼ cup parsley, fetta cheese and 2 tablespoons oil. Mix well to combine. Season with salt and pepper.

Divide the mixture into 12 portions and press firmly on each skewer. Place on a tray and refrigerate while remainder of meal is being prepared.

In a bowl mix together the yoghurt, mint and garlic and set aside.

In a separate bowl, toss together the tomatoes, olives, remaining parsley, vinegar and remaining oil. Add salt and pepper to taste.

Heat an oiled grill plate or barbecue to high and grill the chicken skewers for 5–6 minutes on each side or until golden-brown and firm to the touch.

Serve with the salad and minted yoghurt.

SERVES 4–6

Chicken Korma Pie

1 tablespoon vegetable oil
1 onion, finely diced
3 tablespoons korma paste
500 g chicken mince
20 g plain flour
500 ml chicken stock
300 ml coconut milk
100 g green beans, sliced
¼ cup chopped coriander leaves
salt and freshly ground black pepper
1 sheet shortcrust pastry
1 sheet puff pastry
1 egg, beaten, to glaze

Preheat oven to 200°C. Lightly grease a 20-cm pie dish.

Heat oil in a large non-stick frying pan. Add the onion and korma paste and sauté for 3–4 minutes until fragrant. Add the chicken mince to the pan, stirring with a wooden spoon to break up any lumps. Cook for 10 minutes or until the mince is browned.

Add the flour to the mince and gradually stir in the stock and the coconut milk. Add the green beans and coriander, bring to the boil, reduce heat and simmer for 20 minutes or until sauce thickens. Season with salt and pepper. Leave the mixture to cool completely.

Line the prepared pie dish with the shortcrust pastry. Place in the fridge for 20 minutes.

Pour the pie filling into the dish and place the puff pastry on top. Press the edges together. Brush the top of the pie with the beaten egg.

Place in the preheated oven and cook for 25–30 minutes, until the pastry is golden-brown and crisp. Serve hot or warm.

SERVES 4

Chicken Ravioli

400 g chicken mince
½ cup chopped basil
1¼ cups cream
1 onion, diced
salt and freshly ground black pepper
8 fresh pasta (or lasagne) sheets
    (25-cm × 20-cm)
1 egg, beaten
¼ cup white wine
1 cup grated parmesan cheese

Lightly flour a baking tray.

Place chicken mince, ¼ cup basil, ¼ cup cream, and onion into a food processor. Blend until well combined. Season with salt and pepper.

Lay pasta sheets onto a clean work surface. Using an 8-cm round cutter, cut out 48 rounds.

Divide the chicken mixture into 24 portions and place each portion on a round.

Brush the edge of each round with egg. Place the remaining 24 rounds on top of the chicken mix, pressing around the mixture to make sure there is no air trapped inside. Place the ravioli on the prepared baking tray.

Heat the wine and remaining cream in a large non-stick frying pan. Season with salt and pepper. Add the remaining basil and reduce heat until sauce has thickened slightly (about 2–3 minutes).

Bring a large pot of salted water to the boil. Cook the ravioli in batches for 2–3 minutes at a time. Transfer into the cream sauce and stir until heated through.

Serve topped with parmesan cheese.

SERVES 4

Chicken Cannelloni

450 g chicken mince
1 small white onion, finely diced
2 cloves garlic, crushed
1 cup chopped fresh basil leaves,
*   plus extra for garnish*
salt and freshly ground black pepper
1 × 120-g packet instant dried
*   cannelloni tubes*
30 g grated mozzarella cheese

Béchamel Sauce

700 ml milk
1 bay leaf
70 g unsalted butter
70 g plain flour
freshly grated nutmeg
salt and freshly ground black pepper

Preheat oven to 230°C. Grease a shallow 17-cm × 23-cm baking dish.

To make the béchamel sauce, place the milk and bay leaf in a medium-sized saucepan and bring to the boil. Remove from the heat, discard the bay leaf and set milk aside. Melt the butter in a medium-sized pan, add the flour and cook, stirring with a wooden spoon, for 1–2 minutes. Pour in the hot milk a little at a time, whisking until incorporated. Bring to the boil and cook, stirring constantly, until thick and smooth. Season with nutmeg, salt and pepper.

Combine the mince, onion, garlic and basil in large bowl. Season with salt and pepper and mix well. Fill each cannelloni tube with the chicken mixture. Place tubes in a single layer in the baking dish.

Pour béchamel sauce over the cannelloni and sprinkle with mozzarella. Bake in the oven for 20 minutes, until golden-brown on top.

Garnish with fresh basil leaves and serve.

SERVES 4

Chicken Pasta Bake

2 tablespoons olive oil
1 onion, chopped
2 cloves garlic, crushed
500 g chicken mince
2 teaspoons ground cinnamon
2 × 400-g cans chopped tomatoes
1 bunch English spinach, washed
¼ cup chopped basil leaves
300 g penne pasta, cooked
1½ cups grated cheddar cheese

Preheat oven to 180°C. Grease a 2-litre baking dish.

Heat oil in a large saucepan and sauté the onions and garlic until softened (about 2–3 minutes). Add the chicken mince and cinnamon, stirring using a wooden spoon to break up any lumps.

Add the tomatoes and cook for 45 minutes until the sauce has thickened.

Bring a large pot of water to the boil and blanche the spinach (about 2 minutes). Squeeze out any excess water and roughly chop. Add the cooked spinach and basil to the chicken mixture and season with salt and pepper.

Transfer chicken mix to a large mixing bowl and add the cooked pasta, stir well to combine and pour into the prepared baking dish. Sprinkle with cheese and place in the oven to cook for 25 minutes until the cheese has melted and looks golden.

SERVES 6

Bucatini with Chicken Meatballs

2 slices white bread, soaked in water
500 g chicken mince
¼ cup chopped fresh flat-leaf parsley
500 ml Italian tomato pasta sauce
salt and freshly ground black pepper
2 tablespoons olive oil
500 g dried bucatini
1 brown onion, finely diced
1 clove garlic, finely diced
¼ cup white wine
1 cup grated parmesan cheese
a few black olives, for garnish

Squeeze moisture from the soaked bread, then place in a food processor with the chicken, half the parsley and a tablespoon of the pasta sauce. Season with salt and pepper, then process into a paste. With wet hands, roll mixture into walnut-sized balls.

Heat 1 tablespoon of oil in a large heavy-based pan over medium heat. Cook the meatballs for 3–4 minutes, until well browned. Remove meatballs from the pan and set aside.

Bring a large saucepan of salted water to the boil and cook pasta until al dente.

Meanwhile, heat the remaining tablespoon of oil in the heavy-based pan and sauté the onion and garlic until softened. Add the wine and remaining pasta sauce and bring to the boil. Simmer for 2 minutes, then add meatballs and remaining parsley to the pan and heat until warmed through.

To serve

Drain the pasta and divide between four bowls. Spoon the meatball sauce over the pasta, sprinkle with parmesan cheese and a few olives.

SERVES 4

Chicken Tacos

2 tablespoons oil
1 onion, chopped
2 teaspoons ground chilli
1 teaspoon ground cumin
1 teaspoon garlic powder
1 teaspoon ground paprika
2 teaspoons salt
½ teaspoon cayenne pepper
2 teaspoons onion powder
500 g chicken mince
1 × 400-g can chopped tomatoes
½ cup chicken stock
1 × 135-g packet taco shells
   (12 shells)
1 cup sour cream
3 tomatoes, diced
2 cups grated tasty cheese
iceburg lettuce, shredded, to serve

Preheat oven to 180°C. Line a baking tray with baking paper.

Heat oil in a large saucepan over medium heat. Add the onion and sauté until softened (about 2 minutes). Add the chilli, cumin, garlic powder, paprika, salt, cayenne pepper and onion powder. Cook for 2 minutes until fragrant. Add the chicken mince and stir using a wooden spoon to break up any lumps. Cook for 10 minutes. Add the tomatoes and stock reduce heat and simmer for a further 20 minutes until thickened.

Place the taco shells on the prepared tray and place in the oven for 5 minutes to warm through.

To serve

Place chicken mixture in a serving dish, the sour cream, tomatoes, cheese and lettuce in separate bowls and serve so tacos can be assembled individually.

SERVES 4–6

Chicken Koftas with Rice Pilaf

1 tablespoon olive oil

1 brown onion, chopped

1 clove garlic, crushed

2 teaspoons ground cumin

1 teaspoon ground allspice

1 teaspoon ground cinnamon

500 g chicken mince

½ cup dry breadcrumbs

1 egg, lightly whisked

3 tablespoons chopped coriander
    leaves

salt and freshly ground black pepper

12 bamboo skewers, soaked
    for 30 minutes

natural yoghurt, to serve

Pilaf

40 g butter

1 tablespoon olive oil

1 brown onion, finely chopped

1 cup long-grain rice, rinsed

2 cups vegetable stock

½ cup sultanas

Heat oil in a non-stick frying pan over medium heat. Add onion and garlic and sauté until softened (about 2–3 minutes). Add cumin, allspice and cinnamon. Cook until fragrant (about 3–4 minutes). Leave to cool slightly.

In a large bowl add the chicken mince, onion and spices, breadcrumbs, egg and coriander. Mix well until combined. Season with salt and pepper.

Divide mixture into 12 even portions and shape around each skewer to form slightly flattened sausages. Place the skewers on a tray and refrigerate until the rice pilaf is ready.

To prepare the rice pilaf, heat butter and oil in a large saucepan. Add onion and sauté for 3 minutes until softened. Add rice and stir to coat. Add stock and sultanas to the pan and bring to the boil. Cover and reduce heat to low. Cook for 25 minutes until rice is tender and stock has been absorbed.

Heat an oiled grill plate or barbecue to medium-high and grill the koftas for 5–6 minutes on each side or until they turn golden-brown.

Serve with the rice pilaf and yoghurt on the side.

SERVES 4–6

Honey Mustard Chicken Patties

500 g chicken mince
1 red onion, finely diced
1 tablespoon wholegrain mustard
2 tablespoons honey
½ cup dry breadcrumbs
¼ cup chopped fresh flat-leaf parsley
salt and freshly ground black pepper
2 tablespoons olive oil

Preheat oven to 180°C. Line a baking tray with baking paper.

In a large bowl add the chicken mince, onion, mustard, honey, breadcrumbs and parsley. Season with salt and pepper. Mix thoroughly until combined.

Divide the mixture into four even portions and with damp hands, shape into patties.

Heat oil in a large non-stick frying pan, and cook the patties for 3–4 minutes on each side until golden-brown. Place the patties on the prepared baking tray and cook in the oven for a further 10 minutes or until golden and firm to the touch.

To serve

Serve with vegetables or a salad.

SERVES 4

Chicken Flautas

2 tablespoons vegetable oil
1 onion, chopped
2 cloves garlic, crushed
400 g chicken mince
salt and freshly ground black pepper
200 g fetta cheese, crumbled
8 flour tortillas
tomato salsa, to serve
guacamole (page 53), to serve

Heat 1 tablespoon oil in a large non-stick frying pan to medium heat. Add the onion and garlic and sauté until softened (about 2 minutes). Add the chicken mince, stirring with a wooden spoon to break up any lumps. Cook for 10 minutes until chicken has browned. Season with salt and pepper. Remove from the heat and stir in the fetta cheese.

Warm the tortillas in the microwave on HIGH for 1 minute so they can be rolled without breaking. Place the tortillas on a clean work surface and divide the mixture evenly between them. Roll up each tortilla tightly to make a cylinder shape and secure at each end with toothpicks.

Heat remaining oil on high heat in a large saucepan for deep-frying. Place the flautas, in batches, carefully in the oil and fry for 3–5 minutes until golden and crisp. Place on a tray lined with paper towel to drain excess oil. Repeat until all flautas are cooked.

Serve with tomato salsa and guacamole.

SERVES 4

Stir-fry Chilli Chicken

2 tablespoons peanut oil
500 g chicken mince
2 cloves garlic, crushed
1 tablespoon ginger, grated
2 tablespoons fish sauce
1 long fresh red chilli, finely chopped
1 bunch Chinese broccoli, chopped
1 bunch spring onions, chopped into
    5-cm lengths
1 cup bean sprouts
½ cup roughly chopped mint leaves,
    plus extra for garnish
½ cup roughly chopped coriander
    leaves, plus extra for garnish
½ cup freshly squeezed lime juice
steamed rice, to serve

Heat oil in a wok over high heat, and stir-fry the chicken mince until browned.

Stir through the garlic and ginger. Add the fish sauce and chilli. Add the Chinese broccoli, spring onions and bean sprouts, stir-fry for 1 minute.

Stir through the mint and coriander leaves and then the lime juice.

Serve with hot steamed rice and garnish with herbs.

SERVES 4

Thai Chicken Meatballs

500 g chicken mince
2 kaffir lime leaves, finely shredded
1 fresh red chilli, finely chopped
1 tablespoon fish sauce
2 tablespoons tamarind paste
2 cloves garlic, crushed
¼ cup chopped mint leaves
3 spring onions, thinly sliced
1 tablespoon soft brown sugar
2 tablespoons vegetable oil
steamed rice, to serve
lime wedges, to serve

Preheat oven to 190°C.

Place all the ingredients except the vegetable oil, rice and limes, in a large bowl and mix well to combine.

Roll tablespoonfuls of the mixture into balls and set aside on a plate.

Heat oil to medium-high heat in a large ovenproof dish. Brown the meatballs on all sides (about 3–4 minutes). Place dish in the preheated oven for 10 minutes until meatballs are cooked through.

To serve

Serve with steamed rice and lime wedges.

SERVES 4

Pork

Pork & Green Bean Salad

300 g green beans, sliced
2 tablespoons vegetable oil
1½ tablespoons red curry paste
300 g pork mince
2 stems lemongrass, finely chopped
1 tablespoon fish sauce
½ tablespoon soft brown sugar
3 spring onions, chopped

Bring a saucepan of water to the boil and blanche the beans, drain and refresh under cold water. Set aside

Heat oil in a wok over high heat and cook the curry paste for 1 minute, until fragrant.

Add the pork mince and lemongrass and cook for 5 minutes. Then add the fish sauce and sugar and cook for 1 minute.

Remove from heat, stir through the beans and spring onions and serve.

SERVES 4

Pork Meatballs in Noodle Soup

400 g pork mince
¼ cup chopped coriander leaves
2 spring onions, finely chopped
1 egg
1 tablespoon vegetable oil
1 tablespoon grated ginger
2 cloves garlic, crushed
1 stem lemongrass, finely chopped
2 long fresh red chillies,
    deseeded and chopped
2 tablespoons tamarind paste
6 cups chicken stock
1 tablespoon fish sauce
1 tablespoon sugar
1½ tablespoons freshly squeezed
    lime juice
100 g green beans, sliced
1 × 425-g can baby corn, chopped
250-g packet rice stick noodles

In a bowl add the pork mince, coriander, spring onions and egg, mix thoroughly to combine. Roll tablespoonfuls of mixture into balls.

Cook noodles according to packet directions. Set aside.

Heat oil in a large saucepan and add the ginger, garlic, lemongrass, chillies and tamarind paste. Cook for 1 minute until fragrant. Add the stock, fish sauce, sugar and lime juice. Bring to the boil, reduce heat and simmer for 5 minutes. Add the meatballs and cook for 10 minutes. Add the beans and corn and cook for a further 5 minutes until dumplings are cooked through.

To serve

Divide noodles into four large serving bowls. Pour soup, vegetables and meatballs onto the noodles and serve.

SERVES 4

Spicy Pork with Peas

2 tablespoons vegetable oil

1 onion, chopped

1 clove garlic, chopped

½ tablespoon grated ginger

1 tablespoon garam masala

½ teaspoon ground chilli

1 teaspoon ground coriander

1 teaspoon ground cumin

¼ teaspoon ground turmeric

600 g pork mince

2 tomatoes, chopped

¼ cup natural yoghurt

½ cup peas

½ cup chopped coriander leaves

1 cup baby spinach leaves

roti bread, to serve

Heat oil in a large saucepan over medium heat and sauté the onion, garlic and ginger until softened (about 2–3 minutes). Add garam masala, chilli, coriander, cumin and turmeric. Cook for 1 minute until fragrant.

Add the pork mince, stirring with a wooden spoon to break up any lumps. Cook for 10 minutes until pork has browned. Add the tomatoes, yoghurt, peas, coriander and spinach and cook for a further 2–3 minutes.

Serve with warm roti bread.

SERVES 4

Rustic Pork Terrine

350 g rindless rashers bacon
700 g baby spinach leaves
1 tablespoon olive oil
1 red onion, finely chopped
3 cloves garlic, finely chopped
1 kg pork mince
1 tablespoon pink or green
    peppercorns
½ teaspoon ground allspice
½ teaspoon grated nutmeg
2 tablespoons dry sherry or brandy
1 egg, lightly beaten
salt and freshly ground black pepper
crusty French bread, to serve

Preheat oven to 170°C.

Line a 1-kg casserole dish with the bacon rashers, letting them overhang the sides so they can be wrapped across the top of the terrine mixture.

Rinse spinach well, place in a large saucepan over medium heat and cook in its own juices for 1 minutes or until wilted. Drain, pressing out as much moisture as possible. Set aside.

Heat oil in a frying pan over medium heat. Add onion and garlic and cook, stirring, for 1–2 minutes.

Place pork mince in a bowl with the cooked spinach, onion and garlic, and the peppercorns, spices, sherry and egg. Season with salt and pepper. Mix well, then pack into prepared dish. Fold bacon slices over top and cover with aluminium foil. Place in a baking dish to come halfway up sides of the terrine. Bake in preheated oven for 2 hours.

Remove terrine from oven and allow to cool a little. Leaving it in the dish, place a weight on top and refrigerate overnight.

To serve

To serve, unmould from the dish and cut in slices.

SERVES 8–10

Pork with Thai basil

2 fresh red chillies, chopped
2 cloves garlic, chopped
3 tablespoons vegetable oil
500 g pork mince
1½ tablespoons sugar
⅓ cup fish sauce
1 bunch Thai basil leaves, torn
steamed rice, to serve

In a mortar and pestle grind together the chilli and garlic into a paste.

Heat oil in a large frying pan over medium heat and cook the chilli-garlic paste until it starts to turn brown. Add the pork mince to the pan and cook for 10 minutes until the pork has browned.

Stir through the sugar and fish sauce and add the Thai basil. Mix well to combine.

Serve with steamed rice.

SERVES 4

Thai Omelette with Pork

2 eggs
3 spring onions, finely sliced
1 tomato, finely chopped
1 teaspoon salt
½ teaspoon fish sauce
1 tablespoon oil
1 clove garlic, crushed
50 g pork mince

Whisk the eggs in a bowl and add the spring onions, tomato, salt and fish sauce.

Heat oil in a wok over high heat, add the garlic and pork mince and stir-fry for 1 minute until pork has browned.

Pour in the egg mixture and spread around the wok, reduce the heat and cook for 1 minute, until golden. Gently turn omelette over and cook the other side for a further minute until golden.

Turn onto a place, slice and serve.

SERVES 1 (OR 2 AS LIGHT MEAL)

Grilled Pork Satay

400 g pork mince

1 clove garlic, crushed

1 teaspoon grated ginger

3 tablespoons desiccated coconut

1 fresh green chilli, finely chopped

2 tablespoons freshly squeezed lime
juice

1 tablespoon soft brown sugar

12 small bamboo skewers, soaked
for 30 minutes

Satay Sauce

1 tablespoon oil

½ onion, finely diced

2 cloves garlic, chopped

2 long fresh red chillies, deseeded,
chopped

½ cup roughly chopped raw peanuts

2 tablespoons soft brown sugar

¼ cup coconut milk

In a large bowl combine pork mince, garlic, ginger, coconut, green chilli, lime juice and brown sugar. Divide into 12 portions and shape onto the skewers.

To make the satay sauce heat oil in a medium-sized saucepan over medium heat and sauté the onion, garlic and chilli until softened (about 2–3 minutes). Transfer to a food processor and add the peanuts, brown sugar and ½ cup water. Blend until combined, leaving slightly chunky. Transfer back in to the saucepan and add the coconut milk, return to the heat and keep warm. Add a little more water if the sauce is too thick.

Heat an oiled grill plate or barbecue to high and grill the pork skewers for 5–6 minutes on each side or until golden-brown.

To serve

Serve with the satay sauce and a side salad.

SERVES 4–6

Eggplant Stuffed with Pork

2 eggplants
¾ cup olive oil
1 onion, finely diced
1 clove garlic, crushed
¼ cup chopped fresh flat-leaf parsley
2 teaspoons ground cinnamon
1 teaspoon ground nutmeg
1 tablespoon finely grated lemon zest
500 g pork mince
½ cup chicken stock
2 tomatoes, finely diced
salt and freshly ground black pepper
¼ cup dry breadcrumbs
natural yoghurt, to serve (optional)

Preheat oven to 200°C. Line a baking tray with baking paper.

Cut the eggplants in half, lengthways, and scoop out the flesh leaving a 5-mm boarder. Chop up the eggplant flesh.

Place the eggplant shells on the prepared tray and drizzle with ¼ cup of oil. Bake for 15 minutes until tender.

Heat ¼ cup oil in a large saucepan over medium heat and sauté the chopped eggplant (about 3–4 minutes). Set aside.

Add the remaining oil to the pan and add the onion and garlic, sauté until softened. Add the parsley, cinnamon, nutmeg and lemon zest. Cook until fragrant. Add the pork mince and stir using a wooden spoon to break up any lumps. Cook for 5 minutes or until pork browns. Add the stock, tomatoes and sautéed eggplant and cook for 15 minutes. Season with salt and pepper.

Divide the mixture into the baked eggplant shells, sprinkle with the breadcrumbs and return to the oven for 20–30 minutes until golden-brown.

To serve

Serve with a salad and yoghurt (if using) on the side.

SERVES 4

Shieftalia (Cypriot Sausages)

1 kg pork mince
1 cup finely chopped onion
½ cup chopped fresh flat-leaf parsley
1 teaspoon ground cinnamon
1 teaspoon ground cumin
1 tablespoon ground black pepper
½ teaspoon salt
freshly squeezed lemon juice,
    to serve

Oil a barbecue and preheat to medium.

In a bowl mix the pork well with all the other ingredients except the lemon juice. Use your hands to form mixture into smallish sausages.

Cook sausages on the preheated barbecue for 15 minutes, turning occasionally.

To serve

Squeeze lemon juice over the sausages before serving with a salad of chopped tomato, cucumber, onion and parsley.

SERVES 5–6

Pork with Rice Noodles & Chinese Broccoli

375-g packet rice stick noodles

1 tablespoon vegetable oil

2 cloves garlic, crushed

1 tablespoon grated ginger

4 spring onions, cut into 3-cm
    lengths

500 g pork mince

1 carrot, cut into thin strips

150 g green beans, sliced

1 bunch Chinese broccoli, chopped

¼ cup oyster sauce

2 tablespoons sweet chilli sauce

¼ cup chopped coriander leaves

Cook rice noodles according to the directions on the packet. Set aside.

Heat oil in a wok over high heat and stir-fry the garlic, ginger and spring onions for 1 minute. Add the pork mince, using a wooden spoon to break up any lumps. Stir-fry for 5–8 minutes until the pork has browned.

Add the carrot, beans, Chinese broccoli, oyster sauce and sweet chilli. Stir-fry for 2 minutes. Add ¼ cup water, noodles and coriander leaves.

Cook for a further 2 minutes tossing well to combine. Serve immediately.

SERVES 4

Beijing Noodles

175 g lean pork mince

1½ tablespoons light soy sauce

3 teaspoons hoisin sauce, plus extra
    to serve

2½ teaspoons sugar

225 g dried thin wheat noodles

¼ cup vegetable oil

2 teaspoons Sichuan pepper

2 cloves garlic, peeled

1½ tablespoons fatty pork mince

2 tablespoons finely chopped spring
    onions

1½ teaspoons crushed fresh ginger

1 cup chicken stock

1 tablespoon cornflour

salt and freshly ground black pepper

Place the lean pork mince in a dish with the light soy and hoisin sauces, and the sugar, and mix well. Set aside for 20 minutes.

Bring 1.5 litres of water to the boil, add the noodles, and return the water to the boil. Add ½ cup cold water, bring the water back to the boil again, then cook the noodles until tender, testing frequently after the first 2 minutes. Drain in a colander and set aside.

Heat oil in a wok over high heat until hazy, add the pepper and garlic, reduce heat to medium-low, and cook for 1½ minutes. Remove with a wire ladle and discard. Increase the heat to high, add the seasoned pork and fat pork minces, and stir-fry for 3 minutes, until cooked, using a spatula to break up the meat. Add the spring onions and ginger, and stir-fry briefly.

Combine chicken stock and cornflour, pour into wok and cook over high heat, stirring constantly, until thickened. Season to taste with salt and pepper.

To serve

Divide noodles between shallow bowls and spoon sauce over. Dilute hoisin sauce with a little cold water and serve on the side.

SERVES 2–3

Spicy Pork Patties

600 g lean pork mince
5 spring onions, finely chopped
½ cup chopped coriander leaves
3 tablespoons red curry paste
1 teaspoon fish sauce
1 stem lemongrass, finely chopped
3 Lebanese cucumbers
½ cup roughly chopped mint leaves
1 tablespoon sesame seeds
sweet chilli sauce, to serve

Preheat oven to 180°C.

In a large bowl add the pork mince, spring onions, coriander, red curry paste, fish sauce and lemongrass, mix thoroughly to combine. With wet hands shape into eight patties.

Heat oil in a large ovenproof dish and brown the patties on all sides (about 4–5 minutes). Place dish in the oven for 10 minutes until patties are cooked through.

Using a potato peeler, peel the cucumber into thin strips. Place cucumber strips in a bowl and add the mint and sesame seeds and mix well.

To serve

Serve the pork patties with the cucumber salad and sweet chilli sauce on the side.

SERVES 4

Pork Lo Mein

Sauce

1¼ cups chicken stock
1 tablespoon cornflour
1½ tablespoons oyster sauce

Seasoning

2 teaspoons grated fresh ginger
2 cloves garlic, crushed
3 teaspoons light soy sauce
3 teaspoons cornflour
1 teaspoon sugar
pinch of white pepper
1 tablespoon vegetable or peanut oil

Combine the sauce ingredients in a bowl and set aside.

Combine pork mince with the pork seasoning in a bowl, mix well, and set aside for 30 minutes.

Bring 2 litres of water to the boil, add the noodles and cook for about 2½ minutes, until al dente. Transfer to a colander to drain.

Heat 2 tablespoons of vegetable oil in a wok over high heat and stir-fry the prepared vegetables for 2–3 minutes until crisp-tender. Remove and keep warm. Add the pork and stir-fry over high heat until evenly browned, breaking it up with a spatula. Return the vegetables to the wok. Stir the sauce, pour into the wok and stir over the medium heat until it begins to thicken. Transfer to a dish and set aside, keeping warm. Rinse and dry the wok.

Continued >

225 g coarse pork mince

450-g packet fresh thick egg noodles

¼ cup vegetable or peanut oil

1 small onion, cut into narrow wedges

½ red capsicum, deseeded,
    cut into strips

1 stick celery, sliced thinly
    on the diagonal

2 spring onions, cut into 2.5-cm
    lengths

8 fresh oyster mushrooms, halved

⅔ cup sliced bamboo shoots

1 tablespoon sesame oil

1 teaspoon Chinese black vinegar

2 tablespoons oyster sauce

1 teaspoon salt

Immerse the drained noodles in boiling water to reheat, then transfer to a colander and drain well. Heat remaining vegetable oil in the wok and stir-fry the noodles over high heat for 1 minute. Add the sesame oil, vinegar, oyster sauce and salt, and stir-fry until each strand is coated with the seasonings. Return the sauce to the wok and reheat with the noodles, mixing in evenly. Serve in bowls.

SERVES 2–3

Beef & Veal

Chilli Con Carne

2 tablespoons oil

1 brown onion, finely chopped

2 cloves garlic, crushed

2 tablespoons ground cumin

2 teaspoons cayenne pepper

600 g beef mince

4 medium tomatoes, diced

2 tablespoons tomato paste

½ cup beef stock

1 × 400-g can kidney beans, drained
    and rinsed

1 tablespoon chopped jalapenos

salt and freshly ground black pepper

½ cup chopped fresh coriander
    leaves

½ cup sour cream

corn tortillas, toasted, to serve

Heat oil in a large saucepan over medium heat. Add the onion, garlic, cumin and cayenne pepper and sauté until softened (about 2–3 minutes). Add the mince, stirring with a wooden spoon to break up the lumps. Cook for 5 minutes until the mince browns. Add the tomatoes, tomato paste and stock. Cover with a lid and cook for 40 minutes.

Add the kidney beans and jalapenos and cook uncovered for a further 15 minutes. Season with salt and pepper and stir through the coriander.

To serve

Divide between four serving dishes and serve with a dollop of sour cream and toasted corn tortillas on the side.

SERVES 4

Polpette (Meatball) Sandwich

600 g beef mince
1 onion, finely diced
1 glove garlic, crushed
½ cup finely grated parmesan cheese
2 teaspoons dried oregano
1 egg, beaten
1 cup soft breadcrumbs
salt and freshly ground black pepper
2 tablespoons olive oil
4 panni rolls, cut in half
1½ cups baby spinach leaves
3 tomatoes, sliced
½ cup basil pesto

Preheat oven to 180°C.

In a large bowl add the mince, onion, garlic, parmesan, oregano, egg and breadcrumbs. Season with salt and pepper. Mix thoroughly to combine.

Divide the mixture into eight even portions and roll into balls.

Heat oil in a large ovenproof pan and brown the outside of the meatballs (about 4–5 minutes). Place pan in the preheated oven and cook for 10 minutes.

Warm the panni rolls in the oven and brush both sides with the basil pesto.

To serve

Divide the tomatoes and spinach between the panni rolls. Place warm meatballs on top, allow two meatballs for each sandwich. Serve immediately.

SERVES 4

Cabbage Rolls

600 g beef mince
1 onion, finely diced
1 cup cooked rice
1 tablespoon ground paprika
1 tablespoon caraway seeds
salt and freshly ground black pepper
8 cabbage leaves, core removed
1 × 700-ml jar passata sauce
sour cream, to serve

Preheat oven to 180°C.

In a large bowl add the beef mince, onion, rice, paprika and caraway seeds. Season with salt and pepper. Mix thoroughly to combine. Divide into eight portions. Set aside.

Bring a large saucepan of salted water to the boil. Add 4 cabbage leaves to pan and cook for 1 minute or until softened. Refresh leaves in a bowl of cold water. Drain. Repeat with remaining leaves.

Lay a cabbage leaf out on a clean surface and place one portion of the beef mixture at the top half of the leaf, roll tucking in the sides to make a neat parcel. Repeat with the remaining cabbage leaves and mince mixture. Place cabbage rolls in an ovenproof dish and pour over the passata sauce. Bake in the oven for 25–30 minutes.

To serve

Serve on mashed potato with sour cream.

SERVES 4

Calzone with Bolognese

½ tablespoon active dry yeast

½ cup lukewarm water

200 g plain flour

salt

2½ tablespoons olive oil, plus extra
    for glazing

½ small onion, diced

1 clove garlic, crushed

250 g beef mince

1½ cups passata sauce

½ tablespoon tomato paste

2 tablespoons chopped fresh basil

freshly ground black pepper

50 g grated mozzarella

Combine the yeast and water together in a small bowl. Place the flour and a pinch of salt on a clean work surface making a well in the centre. Pour the yeast mixture and ½ tablespoon oil into the centre and using a fork, combine the flour with the liquid. Knead for 10 minutes, until smooth.

Place the dough in a lightly greased bowl. Cover with a clean tea towel and put in a warm place in the kitchen. Leave for 1½ hours, until doubled in size. Turn the dough out onto the bench and punch out all the air.

Divide the dough into two pieces, place onto a lightly oiled tray. Cover with a tea towel and put in a warm place for 20–30 minutes, until doubled in size.

Meanwhile heat 2 tablespoons oil in a saucepan over medium heat. Add the onion and garlic and sauté until softened (about 2–3 minutes). Add the beef mince and stir with a wooden spoon to break up any lumps. Cook for 5 minutes, or until browned. Add the passata, tomato paste and basil, reduce heat and gently simmer for 30 minutes, until sauce has thickened. Season to taste. Set aside to cool.

Continued >

Calzone with Bolognese (Continued)

Preheat oven to 220°C. Lightly grease 2 × 25-cm pizza trays with oil.

On a lightly floured surface, roll out the dough into 2 × 25-cm rounds and place onto prepared trays.

Spread the bolognese sauce to cover half of each base and sprinkle with mozzarella. Fold the dough over to encase the filling, pinching the edges to seal. Brush each calzone with oil and bake for 15 minutes, or until crisp and golden.

SERVES 2

Murtabak (Malaysian Beef Wrapped in Roti)

½ cup vegetable oil
1 onion, finely diced
2 cloves garlic, crushed
1 tablespoon grated ginger
1 teaspoon ground chilli
1 teaspoon ground cumin
2 teaspoons garam masala
½ teaspoon ground turmeric
1 long fresh green chilli, chopped
400 g beef mince
1 cup vegetable stock
½ cup peas
½ cup thinly sliced green beans
½ cup roughly chopped coriander
    leaves
4 large roti
natural yoghurt, to serve

Heat 2 tablespoons oil in a large saucepan over medium heat. Add onion and garlic and sauté until softened (about 2–3 minutes). Add ginger, chilli, cumin, garam masala, turmeric and green chilli. Cook until fragrant.

Add the beef mince to the pan and stir using a wooden spoon to break up any lumps. Cook for 5–10 minutes. Add stock and cook for another 10 minutes. Stir through the peas, beans and coriander. Cook for a further 5 minutes, adding a little water if the mixture is too dry. (It should be moist but not wet.)

Lay each roti on a clean work surface and divide the beef mixture between them. Fold up each roti to enclose the mixture.

Heat a large non-stick frying pan with the remaining oil over high heat and fry the roti one at a time on both sides until crisp (about 3–4 minutes). Cut each roti into 2–3 pieces.

Serve with yoghurt.

SERVES 4

Swedish Meatballs
with Potato & Dill Salad

700 g small waxy potatoes, peeled,
  chopped
500 g beef mince
1 small onion, grated
½ cup soft breadcrumbs
1 egg, beaten
3 tablespoons chopped dill
salt and freshly ground black pepper
2 tablespoon vegetable oil
½ cup sour cream
1 small red onion, finely diced
2 tablespoons vinegar

Preheat oven to 180°C.

Place the potatoes in a pot of salted cold water and bring to the boil, turn heat down and simmer for 15 minutes or until potatoes are cooked. Drain and set aside to cool.

In a large bowl add the beef mince, onion, breadcrumbs, egg and 2 tablespoons dill. Season with salt and pepper and mix thoroughly to combine. Roll tablespoonfuls of mixture into balls.

Heat oil in a large ovenproof pan over medium heat and brown all sides of the meatballs (about 3–4 minutes). Place pan in the oven and cook for 10 minutes.

Place cooled potatoes in a large mixing bowl and add sour cream, remaining dill, red onion and vinegar. Season to taste and stir well to combine.

Serve the meatballs with a side of potato salad.

SERVES 4

Beef Rissoles with Carrot & Parsnip Mash

600 g beef mince
1 onion, finely diced
½ cup soft breadcrumbs
½ cup tomato chutney
1 small zucchini, grated
salt and freshly ground black pepper
2 tablespoons olive oil
500 g carrots, cut into small pieces
500 g parsnips, cut into small pieces
50 g butter
½ cup milk

Preheat oven to 180°C. Line a baking tray with baking paper.

In a large bowl add the beef mince, onion, breadcrumbs, chutney and zucchini. Season with salt and pepper, mix thoroughly to combine.

Divide the mixture into eight portions and shape into patties.

Heat oil in a large non-stick frying pan over medium heat and brown the rissoles on both sides (about 3–4 minutes). Transfer patties to the prepared baking tray and bake for 10–15 minutes until cooked through.

Place the carrots and parsnips in a large saucepan. Cover with cold water and bring to the boil. Reduce heat and simmer, uncovered, for 15 minutes or until soft. Drain. Return to saucepan. Add butter and milk, season with salt and pepper and mash until smooth.

To serve

Serve the beef rissoles with a side of mash and steamed green beans.

SERVES 4

Red Curry Meatballs

500 g beef mince
1 onion, finely diced
3 tablespoons red curry paste
¼ cup natural yoghurt
salt and freshly ground black pepper
1 tablespoon oil
2 × 400-ml cans coconut milk
2 kaffir lime leaves, shredded
2 cups chicken stock
¼ cup bamboo shoots
1 tablespoon fish sauce
1 tablespoon soft brown sugar
1 × 425-g can baby corn, sliced in
    half lengthways
2 bunches baby bok choy, chopped
1 cup bean shoots
¼ cup chopped coriander leaves
steamed rice, to serve

In a large bowl add the beef mince, onion, 1 tablespoon curry paste and yoghurt, season with salt and pepper and mix thoroughly to combine.

Roll tablespoonfuls of mixture into balls and set aside.

Heat oil in a large saucepan over medium heat and add the remaining curry paste. Stir until fragrant (about 1 minute). Add the coconut milk, lime leaves, stock and bamboo shoots to the pan, bring to the boil and add the meatballs. Reduce heat and simmer for 10 minutes. Add the fish sauce, sugar, corn and bok choy and cook for a further 5 minutes.

To serve

Serve meatballs in bowls, over rice, and top with bean shoots and coriander.

SERVES 4

Korokke (Japanese Croquettes)

3 medium potatoes, peeled and cut
   into pieces
1 tablespoon vegetable oil
½ onion, finely chopped
250 g beef mince
salt and freshly ground black pepper
1 daikon (white radish), grated
1 tablespoon sesame seeds
¼ red cabbage, shredded
1 small red onion, finely sliced
2 tablespoons white wine vinegar
1 egg, beaten
plain flour, to coat
panko crumbs, to coat
vegetable oil, for deep frying

Place potatoes in a large saucepan. Cover with cold water and bring to the boil. Reduce heat and simmer, uncovered, for 15 minutes or until soft. Drain and mash the potatoes while they are hot.

Heat oil in a frying pan over medium heat and sauté the onion until softened. Add the beef mince and cook for 5 minutes. Transfer to a large bowl and add the mashed potato. Season with salt and pepper and leave to cool.

In a large bowl mix together the daikon, sesame seeds, cabbage, red onion and vinegar. Set aside.

Once mince and potato mixture has cooled, shape into flat oval-shaped patties.

Place the egg, flour and panko crumbs in separate bowls. Lightly dust each patty with flour, dip into the egg, and then coat with the panko crumbs.

Heat oil in a large saucepan over high heat for deep-frying. Place a few croquettes carefully in the oil and deep-fry until golden-brown all over. Drain on paper towel. Repeat with the remaining croquettes.

Serve with the daikon salad.

SERVES 4

Family Meatloaf

750 g extra-lean beef mince
2 cups soft breadcrumbs
2 eggs, lightly beaten
1 carrot, grated
1 zucchini, grated, excess moisture
   drained
½ cup peas
2 tablespoons chopped fresh flat-leaf
   parsley
salt and freshly ground black pepper
tomato chutney, to serve

Preheat oven to 180°C. Grease a 11-cm × 21-cm loaf pan.

In a large bowl add beef mince, breadcrumbs, eggs, carrot, zucchini, peas and parsley. Mix thoroughly to combine. Season with salt and pepper.

Press the mixture into the prepared pan. Cover with aluminium foil and bake for 30 minutes.

Remove the foil and bake for a further 20 minutes until browned and cooked through.

To serve

Serve with tomato chutney and a side salad.

SERVES 4–6

Beef Burritos

2 tablespoons vegetable oil

1 onion, finely diced

2 cloves garlic, crushed

1 teaspoon ground chilli

1 teaspoon ground paprika

1 teaspoon ground cumin

1 teaspoon ground coriander

500 g beef mince

1 × 400-g can chopped tomatoes

½ cup beef stock

2 tablespoons chopped oregano
   leaves

¼ cup chopped coriander leaves

8 flour tortillas

1 cup grated cheddar cheese

1 cup sour cream

3 spring onions, chopped

Preheat oven to 200°C.

Heat oil in a large non-stick frying pan over medium heat. Add onion and garlic and sauté until softened. Add chilli, paprika, cumin, and coriander. Stir until fragrant. Add the beef mince, stirring with a wooden spoon to break up any lumps. Cook for 5 minutes until beef browns. Add tomatoes and stock, reduce heat and simmer for 15 minutes, until sauce thickens.

Stir in the oregano and coriander leaves.

Place the tortillas on a clean surface.

Divide the mixture between the tortillas, roll up to enclose the filling and place in a baking dish. Sprinkle with cheese and bake for 10 minutes until the cheese has melted.

To serve

Serve topped with sour cream and sprinkled with spring onions.

SERVES 4

Meatballs with Tomato & Olive Sauce

750 g beef mince

250 g veal mince

2 cloves garlic, crushed

1½ cups soft breadcrumbs

1 cup grated parmesan cheese

¼ cup chopped fresh flat-leaf parsley

salt and freshly ground black pepper

3 eggs

½ cup olive oil

2 onions, diced

2 × 800-g cans chopped tomatoes

1 cup beef stock

1 cup pitted green olives

2 bay leaves

In a large bowl add beef and veal mince, garlic, breadcrumbs, parmesan and parsley. Season with salt and pepper. Add 2 eggs and mix thoroughly to combine. If the mix feels dry add the other egg.

Roll the mixture with a tablespoon into balls. Place meatballs on a baking tray and set aside.

Heat ¼ cup oil in a large saucepan over medium heat. Add the onion and sauté until softened (about 2–3 minutes). Add the tomatoes, stock, olives and bay leaves. Stir sauce and reduce heat.

Heat remaining oil in a large frying pan over medium heat. Add meatballs, do not overcrowd the pan, and brown meatballs on all sides (about 3–4 minutes). Repeat until all meatballs are cooked and then add them to the tomato sauce. Simmer sauce for 1 hour.

To serve

Serve with pasta or a side salad.

SERVES 4

Mince on Toast

2 tablespoons olive oil

1 onion, chopped

1 clove garlic, crushed

1 carrot, finely diced

2 sticks celery, finely diced

1 bay leaf

500 g beef mince

2 × 400-g cans whole peeled
    tomatoes

1 cup beef stock

2 tablespoons tomato paste

1 loaf crusty white sourdough bread,
    sliced thickly

¼ cup roughly chopped fresh flat-leaf
    parsley

Heat oil in a large saucepan over medium heat. Add onion and garlic and sauté until softened. Add the carrot, celery and bay leaf. Cook for a further 5 minutes until vegetables become soft.

Add the beef mince and stir using a wooden spoon to break up any lumps. Cook for 5 minutes until beef browns. Add the tomatoes, stock and tomato paste. Reduce heat and simmer for 45 minutes until the sauce has thickened and the meat is tender.

To serve

Toast the sourdough, place on plates and spoon mince over the top. Serve garnished with parsley.

SERVES 4–6

Family Burgers

1 kg beef mince

2 cups sausage mince (or use Italian
   pork sausages)

1 onion, grated

1 teaspoon ground nutmeg

½ teaspoon ground cloves

1 teaspoon mixed dried herbs

salt and freshly ground black pepper

sliced buns, to serve

lettuce, to serve

tomatoes, sliced, to serve

tasty cheese, sliced, to serve

fried onions, to serve

chutney or tomato sauce, to serve

Oil barbecue and preheat to medium-hot.

Mix both minces with the onion – best done with your hands. Add spices, herbs, and salt and pepper to taste. Shape into thick patties.

Place burgers on preheated barbecue plate and press flat. Cook for 5 minutes on each side, or until done to your liking.

To serve

Serve each patty in a sliced bun with lettuce, tomatoes, fried onions, cheese, chutney or tomato sauce and hot chips.

SERVES 4–6

Bolognese Ragu

2 tablespoons olive oil
1 tablespoon butter
2 cloves garlic, crushed
2 red onions, diced
1 large carrot, peeled and diced
2 sticks celery, diced
1 kg beef mince
500 g pork mince
1 cup milk
salt and freshly ground black pepper
freshly grated nutmeg
1 cup dry white wine
400 g canned chopped tomatoes
grated parmesan cheese, to serve

Heat oil and butter over medium heat in a large, non-stick frying pan. Add garlic and onion, and sauté for 4–5 minutes until softened. Add carrot and celery and sauté for a few more minutes, stirring, until they start to soften.

Add meat in batches and sauté until browned all over. Return to pan, season with a little salt, pepper and some grated nutmeg, then add milk and continue to cook until the liquid has evaporated. Add white wine and stir again, then cook until the wine has reduced.

Add chopped tomatoes, stir well, then simmer over a very low heat, uncovered, for 2–3 hours. Stir occasionally, adding a little extra water if the sauce is getting too dry.

To serve

Serve with your favourite pasta, with freshly grated parmesan on the side.

SERVES 6

Red Capsicums Stuffed with Beef & Pine Nuts

6 small to medium-sized red
   capsicums
chopped fresh basil, to serve

Stuffing

2 tablespoons olive oil
1 medium-sized onion, diced
250 g lean beef mince
90 g short-grain rice, rinsed
1 tomato, chopped
2 tablespoons chopped fresh flat-leaf
   parsley
½ teaspoon ground allspice
½ teaspoon ras al hanout
½ cup pine nuts, toasted
salt and freshly ground black pepper

Sauce

1 tablespoon olive oil
1 red onion, diced
2 cups tomato passata
2 tablespoons tomato paste
3–4 fresh basil leaves

Slice the stem end off each capsicum, and remove seeds and membranes.

To make stuffing, heat oil in a frying pan and sauté onion for a few minutes until soft. Add the beef mince and cook for 5 minutes, stirring occasionally, until lightly browned. Remove from heat and add rice, tomato, parsley, spices and pine nuts. Season with salt and freshly ground pepper.

Preheat oven to 180°C.

To make the sauce, heat oil in a frying pan, sauté onion for 4–5 minutes or until soft, then add tomato passata and paste, and fresh basil leaves. Simmer for 5 minutes, then pour into a casserole dish large enough to hold the capsicums upright (they should fit together snugly).

Spoon stuffing into the capsicums (leave a little space at the top, as the rice will expand when it cooks), and place in the casserole dish on top of the tomato sauce. Cover, place in the preheated oven and cook for 1 hour.

To serve

Place one capsicum per person on each plate, spoon some sauce over and scatter with chopped basil.

SERVES 6

Spaghetti Bolognese

2 tablespoons olive oil

1 medium-sized brown onion, finely
   chopped

2 cloves garlic, crushed

1 medium-sized carrot, diced

2 sticks celery, diced

100 g prosciutto, finely chopped

700 g beef mince

1 cup red wine

½ cup beef stock

700 ml Italian tomato pasta sauce

2 tablespoons freshly chopped
   oregano

2 tablespoons freshly chopped thyme

salt and freshly ground black pepper

500 g dried spaghetti

1 cup grated parmesan cheese

Heat oil in a large heavy-based pan over medium heat and sauté the onion and garlic until softened. Add carrot, celery and prosciutto and cook for 10 minutes or until vegetables are soft. Add mince, breaking up with a wooden spoon and stirring until browned.

Pour in the wine and stock and cook for a further 2 minutes. Stir in pasta sauce, oregano and thyme and bring to the boil. Reduce heat and simmer, uncovered, for 1 hour, stirring occasionally. Season with salt and pepper.

Bring a large saucepan of salted water to the boil and cook the pasta until al dente.

To serve

Drain and divide pasta between four serving bowls. Spoon the bolognese sauce over and sprinkle with parmesan cheese.

SERVES 4

Spicy Beef on Rice Noodles

250 g dried thin rice stick noodles
3 tablespoons vegetable oil
275 g beef mince
2 tablespoons crushed garlic
1 teaspoon freshly ground black
 pepper
2 tablespoons fish sauce
2½ teaspoons dark soy sauce
1 onion, finely sliced
1 tablespoon chopped fresh basil

Sauce

2 cups beef or chicken stock
2 teaspoons Thai red curry paste
2 teaspoons kecap manis (sweet soy
 sauce)
1 tablespoon cornflour

Soak the noodles in warm water for 25 minutes, then drain well and sprinkle with a few drops of the oil to prevent them sticking.

Combine the beef mince with the garlic, pepper, fish sauce and 1 teaspoon soy sauce, and set aside for 15 minutes.

Mix the sauce ingredients in a bowl and set aside.

Heat half the remaining oil in a wok over medium-high heat and stir-fry the onion until softened and lightly golden. Add the beef and stir-fry over high heat until lightly cooked. Add the sauce and cook over low-medium heat, stirring frequently, until very aromatic (about 6 minutes).

In another pan heat the rest of the oil and stir-fry the drained noodles with the remaining soy sauce until each strain is glazed and brown.

To serve

Transfer noodles to a plate. Pour over the sauce, garnish with basil and serve.

SERVES 4

Moroccan Meatloaf

500 g lean beef mince
1 onion, finely chopped
½ red capsicum, finely chopped
1 cup dry breadcrumbs
1 teaspoon ground cumin
1 teaspoon ground coriander
½ teaspoon ground cinnamon
1 egg, beaten
2 tablespoons tomato paste
1 tablespoon chopped fresh flat-leaf
   parsley
1 tablespoon chopped fresh coriander
   leaves
salt and freshly ground black pepper

Preheat oven to 180°C. Line a loaf tin with aluminium foil.

Place all the ingredients in a large bowl and mix well. Put mixture into loaf tin, press down well and cover with more foil.

Stand loaf tin in a shallow baking dish and pour about 4 cm boiling water into dish. Bake loaf for 70 minutes. Take off foil cover, drain off any excess liquid from the tin and then bake for another 10 minutes.

Leave to stand for about 30 minutes before serving or slicing.

SERVES 6

Beef Lasagne

2 teaspoons olive oil
1 brown onion, finely chopped
2 cloves garlic, crushed
750 g beef mince
2 × 400-g cans diced tomatoes
125 ml dry red wine
¼ cup tomato paste
salt and freshly ground black pepper
12 dried lasagne sheets
1 quantity béchamel sauce (page 64)
150 g cheddar cheese, grated
2 cups grated parmesan cheese
60 g mozzarella, coarsely grated
mixed salad leaves, to serve

Heat oil in a large frying pan over medium heat and sauté the onion and garlic until softened. Add the mince, using a wooden spoon to break up any lumps and cook for 5 minutes. Stir in the tomatoes, wine and tomato paste, and bring to the boil. Reduce heat and simmer, uncovered, for 40 minutes, stirring occasionally, until meat is tender and sauce has thickened. Season with salt and pepper.

Preheat oven to 190°C. Grease an ovenproof dish.

Make the béchamel sauce and stir in the grated cheddar and parmesan cheeses.

Spread a quarter of the béchamel over the base of the ovenproof dish. Arrange a single layer of lasagne sheets over the sauce. Top with a third of the mince mixture and then a third of the remaining béchamel sauce. Continue layering with the remaining lasagne sheets, mince mixture and béchamel, finishing with a layer of béchamel. Sprinkle the top with mozzarella. Place dish on a baking tray in the oven and bake for 40 minutes, or until cheese is melted and golden-brown, and the edges are bubbling.

Serve with mixed salad leaves on the side.

SERVES 6–8

Wholemeal Spaghetti with Veal Meatballs

3 tablespoons olive oil

1 medium-sized brown onion, finely
  diced

2 cloves garlic, crushed

2 × 400-g cans chopped tomatoes

50 g sliced ciabatta bread, crusts
  removed and roughly chopped

2 tablespoons milk

500 g veal mince

⅓ cup chopped fresh flat-leaf parsley

1 teaspoon grated lemon zest

1½ cups grated pecorino cheese

50 g sliced mortadella, chopped finely

75 g sliced ham, chopped finely

1 egg, lightly beaten

salt and freshly ground black pepper

500 g dried wholemeal spaghetti

1 cup shaved parmesan cheese

Heat 2 tablespoons of oil in a large heavy-based frying pan over medium heat and sauté the onion and half the garlic, until softened. Add the tomatoes, reduce heat and simmer for 25 minutes.

Meanwhile, combine the bread and milk in a small bowl. Stand for 5 minutes, until the bread has softened.

Preheat oven to 180°C.

In a large bowl combine the soaked bread, mince, remaining garlic, half the parsley, the lemon zest, pecorino, mortadella, ham and egg. Season with salt and pepper and using your hands, mix well. Using wet hands, shape the mixture into 24 balls.

Heat remaining oil in a non-stick frying pan. Add meatballs and cook until browned on all sides. Transfer to a roasting tray and bake in the oven for 10 minutes. Remove meatballs from oven and add to the tomato sauce. Season with salt and pepper. Cook for a further 5 minutes. Stir in the remaining parsley.

While meatballs are cooking, bring a large saucepan of salted water to the boil and cook pasta until al dente.

To serve

Drain pasta and divide between four serving bowls. Spoon the meatball sauce over and scatter with shaved parmesan cheese.

SERVES 4

Veal & Porcini Ragu

40 g dried porcini mushrooms

¼ cup olive oil

20 g butter

1 medium-sized onion, finely diced

1 stick celery, finely diced

1 leek, white part only, finely sliced

1 carrot, finely diced

2 cloves garlic, finely chopped

3 tablespoons roughly chopped fresh
   thyme

1 bay leaf

100 g pancetta, finely chopped

1 kg veal mince

2 teaspoons plain flour

2 tablespoons tomato paste

¼ teaspoon finely grated nutmeg

½ cup red wine

1 cup beef stock

salt and freshly ground black pepper

½ cup milk

¼ cup cream

500 g dried rigatoni

1 cup grated parmesan cheese

Soak the porcini mushrooms in hot water for 15 minutes. Drain and chop finely.

Heat oil and butter in a large heavy-based saucepan over medium heat and sauté the onion, celery, leek, carrot and garlic until vegetables have softened. Stir in the thyme, bay leaf and pancetta and cook for a further 5 minutes. Add the veal mince, breaking it up with a wooden spoon, until browned. Stir in flour and cook for 2 minutes. Add tomato paste, nutmeg and wine, and cook for 3 minutes or until wine has reduced.

Add the porcini mushrooms and half the stock. Season with salt and pepper, reduce heat and cover. Cook for 1 hour, stirring occasionally. Add the remaining stock and milk, cover and cook for a further 30 minutes. Finally, stir in the cream.

Bring a large saucepan of salted water to the boil and cook pasta until al dente. Drain, return to the pan, add the ragu and stir to combine. Serve sprinkled with parmesan cheese.

SERVES 6

Frikkadels (Sri Lankan Meatballs)

500 g beef mince.
½ cup desiccated coconut
½ teaspoon crushed garlic
2 tablespoons grated onion
2 teaspoons finely chopped fresh dill
    or mint
1 tablespoon freshly squeezed lemon
    juice
½ teaspoon salt
½ teaspoon freshly ground black
    pepper
1 egg, well beaten
1 cup dry breadcrumbs
2–3 tablespoons ghee or oil
chutney, to serve

In a bowl knead together the beef, coconut, garlic, onion, dill or mint, lemon juice, salt and pepper until smooth. With wet hands, form into 24 small balls.

Place egg and breadcrumbs in separate bowls.

Dip meatballs into beaten egg and coat with the breadcrumbs.

Heat ghee or oil in a shallow pan over medium heat and fry the meatballs until well browned and cooked through (about 3 minutes). Remove with a slotted spoon and drain on paper towels.

Serve with chutney.

MAKES 24

Lamb

Moroccan Meatball Tagine

500 g lamb mince

1 small onion, grated

¾ cup soft breadcrumbs

½ teaspoon ground cumin

½ teaspoon ground paprika

2 tablespoons finely chopped flat-leaf
   parsley

1 egg, beaten

¼ cup currents

2 tablespoons pine nuts, toasted

salt and freshly ground black pepper

couscous, to serve

Preserved Lemon Sauce

2 tablespoons oil

1 onion, finely diced

½ teaspoon ground paprika

½ teaspoon ground turmeric

½ teaspoon ground cumin

½ teaspoon cayenne pepper

1 preserved lemon, pulp removed,
   chopped

2 cups chicken stock

¼ cup chopped flat-leaf parsley

¼ cup chopped coriander leaves

2 tablespoons freshly squeezed
   lemon juice

2 tomatoes, diced

Preheat oven to 180°C.

To make the meatballs, place the lamb mince, onion, breadcrumbs, cumin, paprika, parsley, egg, currents and pine nuts in a large bowl. Season with salt and pepper. Mix thoroughly to combine. Roll tablespoonfuls of mixture into balls. Set aside.

To make the sauce, heat oil in a large ovenproof dish over medium heat. Add the onion and sauté until softened. Add the paprika, turmeric, cumin and cayenne pepper and stir until fragrant.

Add the preserved lemon, stock, parsley, coriander, lemon juice, tomatoes and the meatballs. Season to taste and bring to the boil. Place covered in the oven for 40–45 minutes.

Serve with couscous.

SERVES 4

Lamb Pizza

2 tablespoons olive oil
1 small red onion, finely chopped
400 g lamb mince
1 teaspoon ground cumin
1 teaspoon ground cinnamon
salt and freshly ground black pepper
2 pieces large Lebanese flatbread
2 tablespoons tomato paste
1 cup baby spinach leaves
80 g fetta cheese, crumbed
1 × 250-g punnet cherry tomatoes,
   halved
½ cup pine nuts, toasted

Preheat oven to 180°C. Line two baking trays with baking paper.

Heat oil in a large saucepan over medium heat. Add the onion and sauté until softened. Add the mince, cumin, and cinnamon. Stir with a wooden spoon breaking up any lumps. Season with salt and pepper to taste.

Place the flatbreads on the prepared baking trays and spread over the tomato paste. Scatter each piece of bread with the spinach, top with the lamb mixture and scatter with fetta, tomatoes and pine nuts.

Place in the preheated oven and bake for 10 minutes until the flatbread is crisp.

SERVES 4

Kousa Mahshi
(Stuffed Zucchini with Lamb)

10 × 12-cm long white zucchini
200 g lamb mince
½ cup long-grain rice
1 tomato, finely chopped
10 g butter, melted
¼ teaspoon ground allspice
¼ teaspoon ground cinnamon
½ teaspoon ground cumin
½ teaspoon ground chilli
¼ cup chopped mint
¼ cup chopped fresh flat-leaf parsley
2 tablespoons olive oil
salt and freshly ground black pepper
¼ cup tomato paste
natural yoghurt, to serve

Remove the stalk end of the zucchini, carefully hollow out the pulp using a small marrow scooper. Wash the shells in a bowl of salted water.

In a large bowl add the lamb mince, rice, tomato, butter, allspice, cinnamon, cumin, chilli, mint, parsley and oil. Season with salt and pepper. Fill each zucchini shell about three-quarters full with the rice mixture. Tap carefully on the bench to settle the filling.

Place the zucchini in a large saucepan. Cover zucchini with cold water. Add tomato paste and 2 tablespoons salt. Bring to the boil and reduce heat to a simmer. Cook for 1 hour or until tender.

Serve in bowls with with some broth and yoghurt.

SERVES 4

Lamb Boreks

400 g lamb mince
100 g goat's cheese, crumbled
3 teaspoons ground paprika
¼ cup chopped mint
1 egg, beaten
salt and freshly ground black pepper
1 × 375-g packet filo pastry
80 g butter, melted
¼ cup sesame seeds
1 cup natural yoghurt
1 clove garlic, crushed
2 tablespoons olive oil

Preheat oven to 180°C. Line a baking tray with baking paper.

In a large bowl add the mince, goat's cheese, 2 teaspoons paprika, mint and egg. Season with salt and pepper and mix thoroughly to combine. Divide into four portions.

Lay one sheet of pastry on a clean work surface, brush with melted butter, lay another sheet on top and repeat twice more.

Place a portion of the mixture at the top right-hand corner of the pastry and fold over on the diagonal. Fold over again and repeat until the end of the pastry is reached. You should have a triangle. Repeat with the remaining pastry and meat mixture.

Place the boreks onto the prepared baking tray. Brush the tops with butter and sprinkle with sesame seeds. Place in the oven for 30 minutes until crisp and golden.

In a bowl mix together the yoghurt, remaining paprika, garlic and oil, season to taste.

To serve

Serve the boreks with the yoghurt mixture and a white bean and onion salad.

SERVES 4

Traditional Shepherd's Pie

1 tablespoon olive oil
1 brown onion, diced
1 clove garlic, crushed
1 medium-sized carrot, diced
2 sticks celery, finely chopped
500 g lean lamb mince
1 tablespoon plain flour
1 cup beef stock
1 bay leaf
1 tablespoon Worcestershire sauce
1 tablespoon tomato paste
1 cup shelled peas, fresh or frozen
salt and freshly ground black pepper
200 g floury potatoes, peeled and
*   quartered*
50 g butter
½ cup milk
melted butter, for glazing
salad leaves, for serving

Heat oil in a large non-stick frying pan over medium heat. Add onion, garlic, carrot and celery, and sauté, stirring, for 5 minutes. Add mince and continue stirring for about 7–8 minutes, or until lamb turns a light brown. Add flour and cook for 2–3 minutes.

Add stock, bay leaf, Worcestershire sauce and tomato paste, and bring to the boil. Reduce heat, cover and simmer for 30 minutes, stirring occasionally, until sauce thickens. Stir the peas through, then test for seasoning.

Meanwhile, cook potatoes in boiling water for 15 minutes, until soft. Drain, and while still warm add the butter and mash well. Stir the milk through until well mixed, then season with salt and freshly ground pepper.

Preheat oven to 180°C.

Spoon mince and vegetables into a wide, 2-litre ovenproof dish. Spread mashed potato over the top, make a pattern with a fork, then brush with melted butter.

Place in preheated oven and bake for 30 minutes until top is golden. Serve with salad leaves.

SERVES 4–6

Lamb Kibbeh

125 g burghul
400 g lamb mince
1 onion, finely diced
salt and freshly ground black pepper
1 tablespoon olive oil
2 teaspoons ground allspice
1 teaspoon ground cumin
¼ cup pine nuts, toasted
vegetable oil, for frying

Cover burghul in cold water and let stand for 15 minutes, drain and squeeze out as much liquid as possible.

In a food processor, add the burghul, 250 g lamb mince, half the chopped onion and season with salt and pepper. Add ⅓ cup ice-cold water and blend until the mixture has a dough-like consistency. Transfer into a bowl, cover and set aside.

Heat oil in a large frying pan and add the remaining onion and sauté until softened. Add the remaining mince, allspice, cumin and pine nuts. Stir using a wooden spoon to break up any lumps. Cook for 5–10 minutes.

Take a heaped tablespoon of the burghul-lamb mixture and roll into an egg-sized ball. With your finger, poke a hole in the ball to make space for the mince and spice filling. Add a teaspoon of filling and pinch the top to seal the ball. Shape the ball into a football shape.

Heat oil in a large saucepan for deep-frying. Place some lamb kibbeh carefully in the oil and deep-fry until golden-brown all over. Drain on paper towel. Repeat with the remaining kibbeh.

To serve

Serve with Lebanese bread and tomato and parsley salad.

SERVES 4

Baked Potato with Lamb

4 medium-sized potatoes

2 tablespoons olive oil

1 onion, finely diced

2 cloves garlic, crushed

350 g lamb mince

1 × 400-g can chopped tomatoes

2 tablespoons tomato paste

¼ cup chopped fresh flat-leaf parsley

¼ cup chopped mint leaves

1 cup grated cheddar cheese

½ cup natural yoghurt

2 tablespoons chopped chives

Preheat oven to 180°C. Line a baking tray with baking paper.

Wrap the potatoes in aluminium foil and place on the prepared tray. Place in the oven for 1 hour, until softened.

Heat oil in large saucepan over medium heat. Add onion and garlic and sauté until softened (about 2 minutes). Add the mince, stirring with a wooden spoon to break up any lumps. Cook for 5 minutes. Add the tomatoes, tomato paste, ½ cup water, herbs. Reduce heat and simmer for 25 minutes until sauce has thickened.

Remove the flesh of the potatoes, leaving a 5-mm boarder. Mix the potato flesh with the mince and divide the mixture between the potatoes. Pack the potatoes firmly, sprinkle the top with cheese and place back in the oven for another 20 minutes until the cheese has melted and the potatoes are warmed through.

To serve

Serve with yoghurt and sprinkled with chives.

SERVES 4

Baby Lamb & Fetta Balls

450 g lamb mince

100 g fetta cheese, crumbled finely

½ tablespoon olive oil

½ red onion, grated or very finely
   chopped

salt and freshly ground black pepper

1 clove garlic, crushed

2 tablespoons finely chopped fresh
   mint or flat-leaf parsley

1 egg, lightly beaten

Onion Marmalade

3 tablespoons olive oil

1 kg red onions, finely sliced

3 tablespoons soft brown sugar

pinch of ground cloves

pinch of ground nutmeg

3 tablespoons balsamic vinegar

salt and freshly ground black pepper

To make the onion marmalade heat oil in a non-stick pan, add onions and 3 tablespoons water, and cook gently for about 10 minutes.

Add sugar, spices and vinegar, stir gently, and cook over low heat, stirring occasionally, for 20 minutes.

When onions are quite soft and any extra moisture is absorbed, season with salt and pepper if needed. Cool completely and set aside.

Oil barbecue and preheat to medium.

Use your wet hands to mix the lamb with all the other ingredients, kneading well to achieve a smooth paste.

Form lamb mixture into marble-sized balls and cook on preheated barbecue plate for about 2–3 minutes on each side.

Serve with the onion marmalade.

SERVES 6–8

Herbed Lamb Burgers with Avocado & Red-onion Relish

500 g lean lamb mince

4 spring onions, finely chopped

2 cloves garlic, finely chopped

1 small fresh red chilli, deseeded and
   finely chopped

3 tablespoons mixed chopped fresh
   mint and flat-leaf parsley

salt and freshly ground black pepper

1 teaspoon ground cumin, roasted

¼ cup soft breadcrumbs

Relish

1 avocado, diced

1 medium-sized red onion, finely
   chopped

1 small Lebanese cucumber, finely
   diced

½ fresh green chilli, deseeded and
   finely chopped

1 tablespoon chopped fresh mint

1 tablespoon freshly squeezed lemon
   juice

salt and freshly ground black pepper

1 tablespoon chopped fresh flat-leaf
   parsley

To make the burgers, mix together the lamb, spring onions, garlic, chilli and half the herbs. Season with salt and pepper to taste, then knead in the cumin and breadcrumbs. Form mixture into eight patties and set aside for 30 minutes.

Oil barbecue and preheat to hot.

Meanwhile, make the salsa by mixing together the avocado, onion, cucumber, chilli, mint, lemon juice and/or sugar if necessary. Season to taste. Finally, add the parsley.

Cook the patties on the preheated barbecue hotplate for 10–15 minutes, turning once.

To Serve

Mix 1 cup Greek-style yoghurt with the remaining herbs, then sprinkle with ground cumin. Serve patties layered into bread rolls with salad leaves and a dollop of the yoghurt.

SERVES 4

Pastitso

250 g dried penne pasta
2 tablespoons olive oil
1 onion, finely diced
2 cloves garlic, crushed
500 g lamb mince
2 × 400-g cans chopped tomatoes
½ cup white wine
½ cup beef stock
2 tablespoons tomato paste
3 teaspoons dried oregano
½ teaspoon ground allspice
½ teaspoon ground cinnamon
salt and freshly ground black pepper

Cheese Sauce

30 g butter
30 g plain flour
2 cups milk
salt and freshly ground black pepper
½ cup grated parmesan cheese

Preheat oven to 190°C. Grease a large baking dish.

Bring a large pot of salted water to the boil, cook the pasta until al dente. Drain and place in the bottom of the prepared baking dish.

Heat oil in a large saucepan to medium heat. Add the onion and garlic and sauté until softened. Add the lamb mince, stirring with a wooden spoon to break up any lumps. Cook for 5 minutes, then add the canned tomatoes, wine, stock, paste, oregano, allspice and cinnamon. Season with salt and pepper, reduce heat and simmer for 1–1½ hours, until sauce has thickened.

To make the cheese sauce, melt butter in a saucepan and add the flour, stir until combined. Whisk the milk in gradually, ensuring there are no lumps. Once all the milk has been incorporated, season with salt and pepper and cook for 5–10 minutes until the sauce thickens.

Stir through the parmesan cheese. Set aside and keep warm.

Once the lamb sauce has cooked pour over the pasta and top with the cheese sauce.

Place in the oven for 45–50 minutes, until the top is golden-brown.

SERVES 6

Pumpkin Gnocchi with Lamb Ragu

3 tablespoons olive oil
1 brown onion, finely diced
1 carrot, finely diced
1 stick celery, finely diced
750 g lamb mince
2 teaspoons ground coriander
1 teaspoon ground fennel seeds
½ teaspoon ground cumin
1 teaspoon freshly chopped rosemary
½ cup red wine
1 × 400-g can diced tomatoes
1 tablespoon tomato paste
1¼ cups chicken stock
salt and freshly ground black pepper
fresh mint leaves, for garnish

Heat oil in a large heavy-based pan over medium heat and sauté the onion, carrot and celery until softened. Add lamb, coriander, fennel, cumin and rosemary and cook, breaking up the lamb with a wooden spoon, until meat has browned. Add the wine, tomatoes, tomato paste and stock, cover and simmer for 1 hour, stirring occasionally. Season with salt and pepper.

While the ragu is cooking, make the gnocchi.

Preheat oven to 180°C.

Place pumpkin on a baking tray and cook in the oven for 25–30 minutes, or until tender.

Meanwhile, steam the potatoes for 15–25 minutes, or until tender. Drain and peel.

Continued >

Pumpkin Gnocchi

*500 g pumpkin, peeled and roughly
    diced*
500 g desirée potatoes
½ teaspoon salt
*300 g plain flour, plus extra
    for dusting*

Pass the pumpkin and potato through a potato ricer or sieve into a large bowl. Season with salt and work in the sifted flour a little at a time until incorporated.

Roll the dough into long logs about 3 cm in diameter, then cut into 2-cm lengths. Place onto a lightly floured clean tea towel to dry.

Bring a large saucepan of salted water to the boil. Boil the gnocchi, in batches, until they rise to the surface, and then for a further minute. Remove with a slotted spoon and keep warm while cooking remainder.

To serve

Place the gnocchi into serving dishes and spoon over the lamb ragu. Garnish with fresh mint leaves.

SERVES 6

Spicy Lamb Samosas

4 large spring roll sheets
1½ tablespoons butter or oil
250 g lean lamb mince (or beef)
1 small onion, very finely chopped
½ teaspoon crushed ginger
½ teaspoon ground turmeric
½ teaspoon ground cumin
½ teaspoon ground chilli
salt and freshly ground black pepper
2–3 tablespoons peas
1–2 tablespoons soft breadcrumbs
2 tablespoons chopped fresh
   coriander leaves or mint
2–3 cups oil

Place spring roll sheets between clean tea towels to thaw.

Heat the butter or oil in a frying pan or wok and sauté mince, onion and ginger until meat is lightly browned. Add spices and seasoning and cook for 1 minute, stirring.

Add peas and ⅓ cup water and simmer, stirring occasionally, for 5–6 minutes until peas are tender and the liquid absorbed. Sprinkle in the breadcrumbs and herbs and stir.

Working one sheet of pastry at a time cut into three even sized strips and fold bottom end of strip over to form a triangle.

Add 2–3 teaspoons of filling and fold up the pastry to form a triangular shaped samosa, moistening the end flap to stick it down. Repeat with remaining sheets and mixture.

Heat oil to medium-high and fry samosas to golden-brown.

MAKES 24

Keema Matter (Lamb with Peas)

3 tablespoons ghee or oil

3 cloves

1 cinnamon stick

8 black peppercorns

1 medium-sized onion, finely chopped

2 cloves garlic, chopped

1-cm piece fresh ginger, chopped

400 g lamb mince

1–2 fresh green chillies, deseeded
     and chopped

½ teaspoon ground turmeric

1 teaspoon garam masala

1 teaspoon ground cumin

1 cup canned crushed tomatoes

1 cup frozen peas

salt

freshly squeezed lemon juice

chopped fresh coriander or mint
     leaves

Heat the ghee or oil in a saucepan over medium heat and fry the cloves, cinnamon and peppercorns for about 30 seconds. Add the onion and fry, stirring frequently, until lightly browned.

Add the garlic, ginger and lamb to the pan and increase the heat, stirring for 2–3 minutes until the meat is lightly coloured. Still on high heat, add the chillies and spices and stir for a few seconds. Add the tomatoes, bring to the boil, then reduce heat and simmer for 2 minutes.

Add the peas and 1 cup water and simmer until peas are tender and the liquid has reduced (about 10 minutes). Season to taste with salt and lemon juice, and stir in chopped coriander or mint before serving.

SERVES 4–6

Lamb Koftas in a Mild Curry

Koftas

1 large onion, chopped

3 cloves garlic, chopped

1½ teaspoons salt

1 tablespoon garam masala, plus
    extra for garnish

½ teaspoon ground cinnamon

3–4 fresh coriander or mint sprigs

1 kg lamb mince

peanut or vegetable oil, for deep-
    frying

Curry Sauce

2 large onions, chopped

4 cloves garlic, chopped

2-cm piece fresh ginger, chopped

1½ tablespoons coriander seeds

1 teaspoon cumin seeds

2 dried red chillies

3 cloves

2 cardamom pods, cracked

To make the koftas, use a food processor to combine the onion and garlic with the spices and herbs until reasonably smooth. Remove half the mixture and set aside.

Add half the meat to the processor and grind to a smooth paste. Remove and then process reserved onion paste and remaining meat to a smooth paste.

Knead the two meat batches together in a large bowl, then with wet hands shape into balls the size of walnuts, and flatten slightly.

Heat oil in a frying pan to medium-hot, and fry the meatballs in batches, until well-browned (about 3–5 minutes). Remove with a slotted spoon and set aside.

To prepare the sauce, process the onions, garlic and ginger to a paste in a food processor and set aside. In a dry pan roast the coriander and cumin seeds with the dried chillies over medium heat until fragrant (about 2 minutes). Tip into a spice grinder and grind to a fine powder. Add the cloves, cardamom and cinnamon and set aside.

Continued >

1 cinnamon stick
⅓ cup ghee or oil
1 cup canned crushed tomatoes
2 teaspoons ground sweet paprika
½ cup sultanas
1 cup natural yoghurt or sour cream
salt
thick cream, to garnish
chopped fresh coriander leaves, to
    garnish
flaked almonds, toasted, to garnish

In a saucepan with a heavy base, heat the ghee or oil and fry the onion paste for about 8 minutes, until lightly coloured. Add the prepared spices and cook a further 2 minutes, stirring, then add the tomatoes and paprika and simmer for 3–4 minutes. Stir in the sultanas and yoghurt or sour cream, and carefully add the meatballs and any liquid from their bowl. Add salt to taste. Simmer gently until the sauce is very creamy and aromatic, and the meatballs are heated through.

To serve

Transfer koftas to a serving dish. Garnish with a swirl of the thick cream, and a sprinkling of garam masala, chopped herbs and toasted almonds.

SERVES 6–8

Sweets

Christmas Mince Pies

2 tablespoons soft brown sugar

2 tablespoons brandy

1 small Granny Smith apple, peeled, grated

85 g raisins, chopped

85 g currants

85 g sultanas

60 g dried cranberries

⅓ cup marmalade

1 teaspoon mixed spice

185 g chilled butter, chopped

⅓ cup icing sugar

1 tablespoon finely grated orange zest

2¼ cups plain flour

1 egg yolk

caster sugar

icing sugar, for dusting (optional)

In a large bowl add the brown sugar, brandy, apple, raisins, currants, sultanas, cranberries, marmalade and mixed spice. Stir, cover and set aside overnight.

Place the butter, icing sugar, zest and flour in a food processor and blend until mixture resembles fine breadcrumbs. Add the egg yolk and 2 tablespoons cold water, and blend until the dough just comes together.

Turn the dough onto a lightly floured surface and knead until smooth. Divide the dough into two balls, one slightly larger than the other and place in the fridge for 1 hour.

Preheat oven to 180°C. Grease 2 × 12-hole patty pans.

Roll the larger piece of dough between two sheets of baking paper until 3-mm thick.

Cut out 24 rounds with a 6.5-cm cutter. Press the rounds into the patty pans and prick the bases with a fork. Return to the fridge for 20 minutes.

Place pastry bases in the oven and bake for 10 minutes until golden-brown. Let cool in the pans.

Continued >

Christmas Mince Pies (Continued)

Roll the remaining dough between two sheets of baking paper until 3-mm thick. Using a 4.5-cm star shaped cutter, cut 24 stars.

Spoon the fruit mix into the pastry cases, pressing mixture in firmly. Top with the stars pressing edges to seal.

Sprinkle top of pies with caster sugar and bake in the oven for 10–15 minutes until golden.

Transfer onto a wire rack. Once the mince pies have cooled, dust with icing sugar (if using).

MAKES 24

Mince Slice

2 cups mixed dried fruit

2 tablespoons freshly squeezed orange juice

¼ cup soft brown sugar

2 teaspoons ground cinnamon

1 teaspoon ground allspice

185 g chilled butter, chopped

½ cup caster sugar

1 egg

1 tablespoon finely grated orange zest

1½ cups plain flour, sifted

1 cup self-raising flour, sifted

icing sugar, for dusting

Preheat oven to 180°C. Grease a 22-cm round tin and line with baking paper.

In a medium saucepan add the mixed fruit, orange juice, sugar, cinnamon and allspice, stirring occasionally for 5 minutes or until sugar is melted and mixture just comes to the boil. Set aside to cool completely.

Meanwhile, place butter, sugar, egg, orange zest and flours in a food processor. Blend until dough forms. Transfer dough to a lightly floured surface. Knead until smooth. Cut dough in half. Press one half of dough into the prepared tin.

Spread the fruit filling over the base. Roll out remaining dough until large enough to cover filling. Place over filling and prick with a fork.

Place in the oven and bake for 25–30 minutes.

Dust with icing sugar and cut into wedges to serve.

SERVES 6–8

Christmas Ice-cream Pudding

2 tablespoons soft brown sugar

2 tablespoons brandy

85 g raisins, chopped

85 g currants

85 g sultanas

60 g dried cranberries

60 g glace cherries

100 g dried figs, chopped

⅓ cup marmalade

1 teaspoon mixed spice

1 litre vanilla ice-cream

toasted almond flakes, to serve

In a large bowl add all the ingredients except the ice-cream. Cover and set aside for 24 hours.

Place the ice-cream in the fridge for a couple of hours until softened. Stir through the fruit mince. Place ice-cream into the freezer overnight.

Serve pudding with toasted flaked almonds.

SERVES 4–6

Steamed Mince Pudding

110 g softened butter
½ cup caster sugar
2 eggs, beaten
220 g self-raising flour
½ cup milk
200 g fruit mince
custard, to serve
ice-cream, to serve

Cream butter and sugar together with a electric mixer. Beat in eggs. Slowly add sifted flour and milk. Fold through the fruit mince.

Put mixture in a greased steamer and place in a saucepan with enough hot water to cover half the steamer. Steam for 1 hour.

Serve with custard and ice-cream.

SERVES 4

Fruit-filled Biscuits

125 g butter
½ cup caster sugar
1 egg
1 tablespoon finely grated lemon zest
2 cups plain flour, sifted
1 teaspoon baking powder, sifted
200 g fruit mince

Preheat oven to 180°C. Grease two baking trays.

Cream the butter and sugar with an electric mixter until light and fluffy. Add the egg and lemon zest and beat well to combine. Add the flour and baking powder and mix well.

Turn out onto a clean work surface and knead. Roll out the dough to 4-mm thickness and using a 7-cm fluted cutter, cut out roughly 20 rounds.

Using a 1-cm fluted cutter, cut a hole out in the middle of half of the biscuits.

Place biscuits on the prepared trays and bake for 10–15 minutes until golden.

Cool on a wire rack. Once cooled spread the fruit mince on the whole biscuits and cover with the holed biscuit.

MAKES ABOUT 20

Apple Mince Strudel

3 small Granny Smith apples, peeled
    and thinly sliced
2 tablespoons freshly squeezed
    lemon juice
150 g fruit mince
150 g soft brown sugar
¼ cup dried cranberries
80 g butter, melted
4 sheets filo pasty
¼ cup roughly chopped walnuts
vanilla ice-cream, to serve

Preheat oven to 180°C. Line a baking tray with baking paper.

In a large bowl add the apples, lemon juice, fruit mince, brown sugar and cranberries. Mix well to combine.

Lay the first sheet of filo pasty on a clean tea towel on your work surface and brush with melted butter. Lay another sheet of filo pastry on top, brush with butter. Repeat with remaining pastry.

Spread the apple mix along the long edge of the filo pastry.

Starting at the edge with the apple mixture, gently lift the edge of the tea towel and use it to help you roll the pastry up lengthways, folding in the edges to enclose the filling. Brush with butter and sprinkle with the chopped walnuts.

Place on the prepared tray and bake in the preheated oven for about 20 minutes or until golden-brown.

Serve with vanilla ice-cream.

SERVES 4

Cinnamon Mince Slice

1 cup plain flour, sifted
½ cup rice flour, sifted
⅓ cup caster sugar
125 g cold butter, cut into small
    pieces
2 eggs, separated
400 g fruit mince
2 tablespoons caster sugar mixed
    with 1 teaspoon ground cinnamon,
    for sprinkling

Preheat oven to 180°C. Grease and line a 20-cm × 30-cm lamington tin.

In a food processor, blend the sifted flours, sugar and butter until crumbly. With the motor running, add the egg yolks and blend until a soft dough forms.

Remove dough and knead gently on a lightly floured surface. Press two-thirds of the dough into the tin. Spread fruit mince evenly over the base and then crumble remaining dough over the top.

Beat egg whites until frothy and drizzle over the top. Sprinkle with the cinnamon sugar.

Bake for 20 minutes until golden-brown. Cool before cutting into squares.

MAKES 24

Index